图书在版编目（CIP）数据

趣味汉语拼音课本（基础篇）/蔡云凌,刘德联编.—北京：世界图书出版公司北京公司,2007.4
　　ISBN 978-7-5062-8623-7

　　Ⅰ.趣...　Ⅱ.①蔡...②刘...　Ⅲ.汉语拼音－对外汉语教学－教材　Ⅳ.H195.4

中国版本图书馆 CIP 数据核字（2007）第 017450 号

趣味汉语拼音课本（基础篇）

编　　　者:	蔡云凌　刘德联
责任编辑:	杨艳慧　张颖颖
装帧设计:	春天书装图文设计工作室
配　　图:	构思香
出　　版:	世界图书出版公司北京公司
发　　行:	世界图书出版公司北京公司
	（北京朝内大街 137 号　邮编　100010　电话　64077922）
销　　售:	各地新华书店和外文书店
印　　刷:	北京雷杰印刷有限公司
开　　本:	787×1092 毫米　1/16
印　　张:	9
字　　数:	120 千字
版　　次:	2007 年 4 月第 1 版　2007 年 4 月第 1 次印刷

ISBN 978-7-5062-8623-7/H·960　　定价: 35.00（含 1 张 MP3）

版权所有　翻印必究

目 录

第一课　单韵母和声调
Lesson One　Simple Finals and Tones ·················· 1

第二课　声母(一)
Lesson Two　Initials (I) ·················· 9

第三课　复韵母(一)
Lesson Three　Compound Finals (I) ·················· 21

第四课　声母(二)
Lesson Four　Initials (II) ·················· 34

第五课　复韵母(二)
Lesson Five　Compound Finals (II) ·················· 48

第六课　第三声的变调
Lesson Six　Third-tone Sandhi ·················· 60

第七课　汉语拼音的音节结构与拼写规则
Lesson Seven　Syllable Structure and Spelling Rules of *Pinyin* ·················· 69

第八课　"一"和"不"的变调
Lesson Eight　Tone Sandhi of "一" and "不" ·················· 83

第九课　卷舌韵母与儿化韵
Lesson Nine　Retroflex Finals and Suffixation of the Nonsyllabic "r" ·················· 92

第十课　轻声
Lesson Ten　Neutral Tone ·················· 104

录音文本与参考答案
Tapescript and Answer Key ·················· 113

前　　言

　　众所周知，学好汉语拼音是学好汉语的先决条件之一。

　　近年来，随着对外汉语教学事业的蓬勃发展，世界上学习汉语的人数逐年增多，大量为初学者编写的汉语教材也如雨后春笋般地涌现出来。但是，它们大都是在初级汉语课本的前面加上几课有关拼音的讲解和练习，既简单又缺乏系统性，专门为外国学习者编写的汉语拼音教材却屈指可数。为此，我们专门为外国学习者编写了《趣味汉语拼音课本》（基础篇），供来华或在海外学习汉语的学习者使用。

　　本书在编写上有以下特色：

　　1. 充分考虑到外国人学习拼音的难点，在教材编写时贯彻先易后难的原则，采取循环往复的教法，进行系统化的讲解。

　　我们凭借多年的教学经验，根据外国学习者学习拼音过程中的难点和习得顺序，将声母、韵母按难易程度切分成几个部分，交叉讲解并进行练习。此外，我们在每一课出现新的知识点时，都与前面所学内容结合起来讲解，从而既学了新的知识，也复习了旧的内容，以循环往复、螺旋上升的方式促进学生进步。

　　2. 注重教材的趣味性，通过大量的图片，将拼音教学形象化，同时使其与汉字认读结合起来，丰富学习内容，引发学习者的积极性。

　　对学习者来说，单纯学习和练习语音是比较枯燥乏味的。我们在课本中加入大量活泼可爱的卡通形象，一方面可以帮助学习者理解相关的语音知识，另一方面也增加了课本对学习者的吸引力，减轻学生在学习过程中产生的疲劳和厌倦感。另外，我们在做音节的讲解与练习时，将拼音、图片、汉字和英文注释结合在一起，这样既可以帮助学习者学习拼音，也可以使学习者掌握一定的汉字和汉语词汇，将拼音学习与汉字学习自然地融合在一起，为以后的学习打下基础。

3. 以练为主，注重讲解的通俗性。

我们在做拼音知识讲解时，尽量使用通俗的语言，并通过简单易懂的图画帮助学习者理解。比如讲解四声的时候，没有标注其音值，因为在教学中我们发现标注音值对学生学习起不到太大的作用。因此我们在书中借用五线谱标出四个声调相对的音高位置，使学生对四个声调的高低差别一目了然。此外，我们在讲解时还通过大量图文并茂的范例加深学习者的理解，并在每一课的课后布置了大量的练习，除了朗读的训练以外，还包括听、说、写这三方面的技能训练。练习形式多样化，有助于学习者掌握已学知识。

本书可作为教授外国学生初学汉语拼音的语音教材，也可作为纠正外国学生的汉语发音的正音教材，同时还可作为中国儿童学习汉语拼音的参考书。

本书在编写过程中，得到世界图书出版公司北京公司郭力女士的指导与启发；北京体育大学音像出版社的刘润芝女士为本书做了英文翻译；美国的 Wen Li Bartholomew 和 John Bartholomew 为本书的英文翻译作了校对，世界图书出版公司北京公司的杨艳慧、张颖颖二位编辑为本书的出版付出了辛勤的劳动，在此一并表示真诚的谢意。

本书编著者按汉语拼音音序排列。

为方便学习者学习，本书配有范读录音 MP3。

编　者
2006 年 9 月

Preface

As we all know, mastering *pinyin* (the system of spelling Chinese characters phonetically using the Roman alphabet) is a precondition of learning Chinese well.

As a result of China's domestic economic growth and international trade in recent years, more and more people in the world are learning Chinese. Plenty of Chinese textbooks for beginners have sprung up like mushrooms; however, the number of *pinyin* textbooks for foreigners can be counted on one's fingers. Most of them consist of a Chinese primary textbook, several additional texts with explanations and exercises of *pinyin*. These textbooks are not only simplistic but also unsystematical. Therefore we present a comprehensive and systematic approach in Interesting Chinese *Pinyin* Textbook for foreigners learning the Chinese language in China and overseas.

This book encompasses the following characteristics:

I. With an eye to the difficulty that foreigners have in learning Chinese, we begin with principles easily learned and graduate to more difficult ones, explaining the principles and contents within the book systematically by circulatory and repetitive teaching methods.

Based on years of teaching experience, we divide the initials and finals into several parts and explain them systematically in the order of difficulty and acquisition foreigners have had in learning them. Moreover, we adopt a cyclical arrangement method when explaining the new language points by banding them with others that appeared in earlier lessons. Therefore, learners review points previously taught while studying new ones, with the result of a spiral growth in knowledge of the Chinese language.

II. This book focuses on maintaining the student's interest. Plentiful pictures, visual teaching aids, and the integration of *pinyin* with Chinese characters enrich the structural content, keeping students engaged with the presented material.

For learners, studying and practicing *pinyin* is boring. Therefore, we incorporated plenty of lively cartoon images, which not only help learners to understand the related phonetic knowledge but also add to the appeal of the textbook by lessening the weariness and boredom of learning. Moreover, we integrate *pinyin*, pictures, and English notes together in the explanations, exercises and pronunciation of Chinese syllables, which helps the learners understand not only *pinyin*, but also Chinese characters and vocabulary, so as to lay a solid foundation for future study.

Ⅲ. This book gives primacy to practice through exercises and to explain utilizing the common language and experiences of everyday life. We try using commonly spoken language and simple, lucid pictures to assist learners in understanding the concepts and principles described in this textbook. For instance, we do not label the phonetic values in explaining the four tones because we have found that the phonetic values do not play an important part in teaching and learning. Therefore, we adopt staves to label the relative positions of the four tones, which, at a glance, present a clear picture of pronunciation. Furthermore, we adopt many examples integrating explanations with pictures to help learners understand the presented material. There are various types of skill practices, such as reading, listening, talking and writing, which assist the learners in grasping knowledge of the basic concepts.

This book can be used either as an introductory *pinyin* textbook for foreigners beginning to learn Chinese, or as a *pinyin* textbook for foreigners desiring to correct and improve their Chinese pronunciation, or as a reference book for Chinese children learning *pinyin*.

We would like to express our deep gratitude to Ms. Guo Li from the Beijing World Publishing Corporation for her suggestions and guidance; to Ms. Liu Runzhi from Beijing Sport University Audio & Video Press for her translation; to our American friends Mrs. Wenli Bartholomew and Mr. John Bartholomew who proofread the translated version; to Yang Yanhui and Zhang Yingying from the Beijing World Publishing Corporation for their editing.

Authors of this book are listed in alphabetical order on the following page.

For one's convenience, this book is available in MP3 format.

Authors
Sep, 9, 2006

第一课　单韵母和声调

Lesson One　Simple Finals and Tones

单韵母（Simple Finals）

说明 1

汉语拼音的单韵母共有 6 个。

【Illustration 1】

There are 6 simple finals in *pinyin*.

说明 2

从 a 到 e 再到 i，是嘴的开口度由大逐渐变小的过程。

【Illustration 2】

From "a" to "e" and then "i", the mouth's opening becomes gradually smaller when pronouncing the finals.

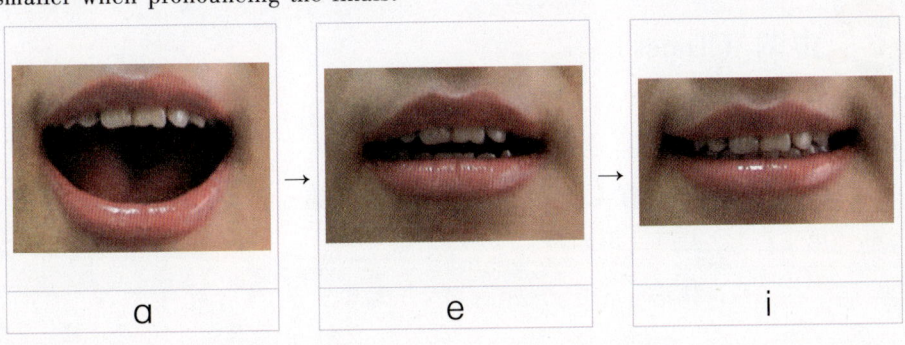

说明 3

先发 i，然后把嘴唇搓成圆形发出的就是 ü。

【Illustration 3】

When pronouncing "ü", first you pronounce "i", and then form the lips into a circle.

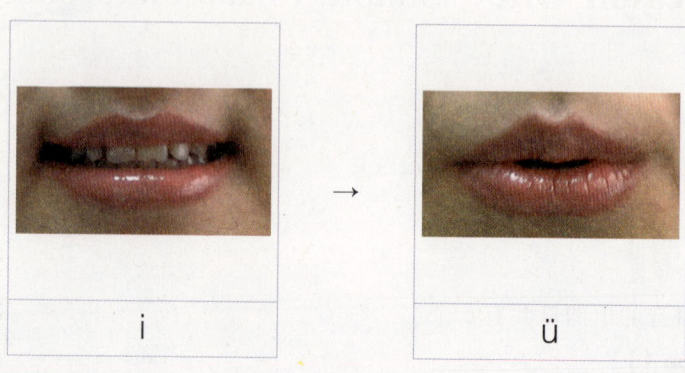

说明 4

在 u 后边加一个发音轻而短的 e 发出的就是 o。

【Illustration 4】

Pronouncing "u" and ending with a light and short "e" will result in the pronunciation of "o".

$$u + e \Longrightarrow o$$

声调 (Tones)

说明 1

汉语拼音的声调共有 4 个，分别为：阴平（第一声）、阳平（第二声）、上声（第三声）、去声（第四声）。

【Illustration 1】

There are four basic tones in Chinese pronunciation: the high and level tone (first tone), the rising tone (second tone), the falling-rising tone (third tone), and the falling tone (fourth tone).

阴平（第一声）	阳平（第二声）	上声（第三声）	去声（第四声）
high and level tone	rising tone	falling rising tone	falling tone
‾	´	ˇ	`

说明 2

在汉语语音中，同一个音节加上不同的声调，意思也会不同。

【Illustration 2】

In *pinyin*, a syllable can have different meanings depending upon which tone it has.

ā	á	ǎ	à
表示叮嘱 (to indicate urge)	表示询问 (to indicate inquiry)	表示惊疑 (to indicate surprise)	表示赞叹 (to indicate admiration)

单韵母的拼写规则（Spelling Rules of Simple Finals）

a、o、e 的拼写（Spellings of "a", "o" and "e"）

说明 3

a、o、e 作为音节独立使用时，只需在上方标出声调。

【Illustration 3】

If "a", "o" or "e" is used as an individual syllable, the tone shall be marked above the letter only.

ā	é	 è	 ò
啊（ah）	鹅（goose）	饿（hungry）	哦（oh）

i、u、ü 的拼写（Spellings of "i", "u" and "ü"）

说明 4

i、u、ü 作为音节独立使用时，其拼写要在前面加上 y 或 w；ü 上面的两个点也要去掉，即 yi、wu、yu。

【Illustration 4】

If "i", "u", or "ü" is used as an individual syllable, "y" or "w" must be placed in front of it. The two dots above "ü" are omitted. Examples：yi, wu, yu.

yī

衣（clothes）

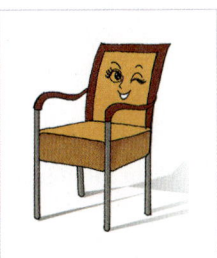

yǐ

椅（chair）

wū

屋（house）

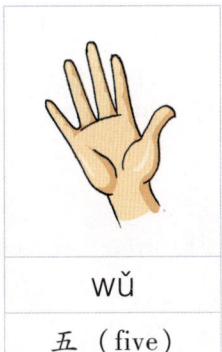

wǔ

五（five）

yú

鱼（fish）

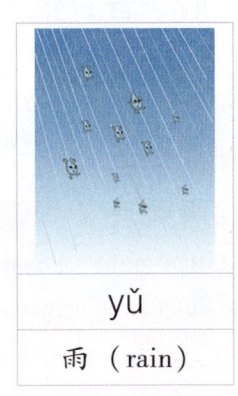

yǔ

雨（rain）

第一课

单韵母和声调

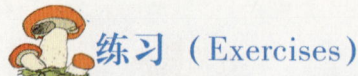 练习（Exercises）

一、听录音，把下面的单韵母按听到的顺序写在空格里：

Listen to the tape and write down in the following blanks the simple finals in the order you hear them.

a   o   e   i   u   ü

二、听录音，给下面的拼音加上声调：

Listen to the tape; add tones to the *pinyin*.

1. o	2. yi	3. yu	4. e	5. a	6. wu
7. yu	8. wu	9. o	10. a	11. yi	12. e

三、听录音，跟读，注意每组拼音的区别：

Listen to the tape and repeat after the tape each group of *pinyin*. Pay attention to the differences between each group.

1. yí yú	2. á ǎ	3. wú wù
4. ě ǒ	5. wù yù	6. yǐ yǔ

四、听录音，按所听到的拼音的顺序在图的下面写上序号：

Listen to the tape and number the following pictures according to the sequence that you hear them.

（一）1~4

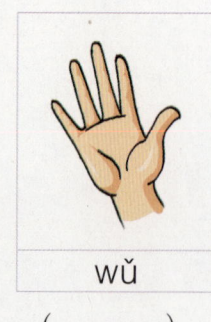
wǔ
(　　)

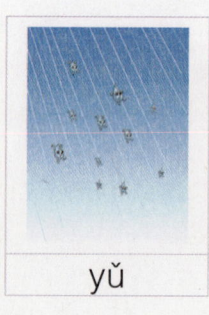
yǔ
(　　)

é
(　　)

yī
(　　)

(二) 5~8

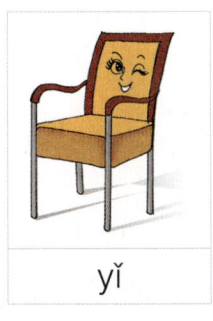
yǐ
(　　)

è
(　　)

wū
(　　)

yú
(　　)

五、朗读下面的拼音：

Read aloud the following *pinyin*.

āyí	èyú	èyì	éyǔ
阿姨	鳄鱼	恶意	俄语
aunt	crocodile	ill intentions	Russian

yǔyì	yùyī	wǔyì	yìwù
语意	浴衣	武艺	义务
meaning of words	bathrobe	skill in *wushu*	duty

yíyì	yìyì	wūyú	wúyì
一亿	意义	乌鱼	无意
a hundred million	meaning	snakeheaded fish	accidentally

六、朗读下面的拼音，体会每组拼音声调的区别：

Read aloud the following *pinyin* and try to distinguish the differences between each group of tones.

yǔyī	yùyī	éyǔ	èyú
雨衣	浴衣	俄语	鳄鱼
raincoat	bathrobe	Russian	crocodile

yīwù	yíwù	yìyì	yíyì
衣物	遗物	意义	疑义
clothing	relic	meaning	doubt

wǔyì	wúyì	yìwù	yíwù
武艺	无意	义务	贻误
skill in *wushu*	accidentally	duty	bungle

七、看图，在图下面的空格里写出相应的拼音：

Look at the pictures; write down the appropriate *pinyin* in the corresponding blank under each picture.

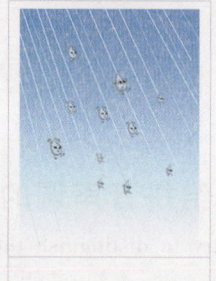
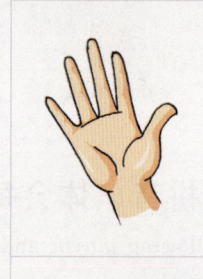

第二课 声母（一）

Lesson Two   Initials（I）

唇音声母（Labial Sounds of Initials）

说明 1

汉语拼音的唇音声母共有 4 个。

【Illustration 1】

There are 4 labial sounds of initials in *pinyin*.

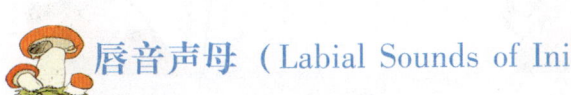

b p m f

说明 2

由于 b、p、m、f 是辅音，在发音的时候，如果不加上元音很难发出音来。所以我们在发这些音时，实际上要在后边加上类似 o 的音。

【Illustration 2】

Initials "b, p, m, f" are difficult to pronounce without adding a final, so we add the sound "o" when pronouncing them.

b → bo p → po m → mo f → fo

说明 3

b 和 p 发音近似，有些初学者很容易将二者混淆。区分 b 和 p 的一个简易的方法是：把手放在嘴前，发 p 时手掌可以感觉到较强的气流，而发 b 时则感觉轻微。

【Illustration 3】

The sound of "b" is similar to that of "p", which many beginners easily confuse. There is a simple method to ensure proper pronunciation of these sounds: place your hand about an inch in front of your mouth; when pronouncing "p", you can feel your breath impact your hand, whereas when pronouncing "b", you have no such feeling.

舌尖声母（一）（Apical Sounds in Initials (I)）

说明 1

汉语拼音的舌尖声母共有 7 个，在这一课中，我们先学其中的 4 个。

【Illustration 1】

There are 7 apical sounds of initials in *pinyin*; we'll learn 4 of them in this lesson.

说明 2

由于 d、t、n、l 是辅音，在发音的时候，如果不加上元音很难发出音来。所以我们在发这些音时，实际上要在后边加上类似 e 的音。

【Illustration 2】

Initials "d, t, n, l" are difficult to pronounce without adding a final, so we add the sound "e" when pronouncing them.

d → de　t → te　n → ne　l → le

说明 3

d 和 t 发音近似，有些初学者很容易将二者混淆，区分 d 和 t 的一个简易的方法是：把一张轻薄的纸片放在嘴前，发 t 时可以明显地看到纸片的摆动，而发 d 时则没有。

【Illustration 3】

The sound of "d" is similar to that of "t", which many beginners easily confuse. There is a simple method to ensure proper pronunciation of these sounds：Place a piece of thin paper in front of your mouth when pronouncing "t"；you can clearly see the paper move, whereas when pronouncing "d", you can't.

 舌根声母（Velar Sounds in Initials）

 说明 1

汉语拼音的舌根声母共有 3 个。

【Illustration 1】

There are 3 velar sounds of initials in *pinyin*.

g　k　h

 说明 2

由于 g、k、h 是辅音，在发音的时候，如果不加上元音很难发出音来。所以我们在发这些音时，实际上要在后边加上类似 e 的音。

【Illustration 2】

Initials "g, k, h" are difficult to be pronounced without adding a final, so we add the sound "e" when pronouncing them.

g → ge　k → ke　h → he

 说明 3

g 和 k 发音近似，有些初学者很容易将二者混淆。区分 g 和 k 可参照区

分 b 和 p、d 和 t 的方法。

【Illustration 3】

The sound of "g" is similar to that of "k", which many beginners easily confuse. For proper pronunciation, you can refer to the methods explaining the differing of "b" from "p" and "d" from "t".

汉语拼音音节的基本结构
(Basic Structure of Syllables in *Pinyin*)

 说明 1

汉语拼音音节的基本结构为：声母+韵母，声调贯穿于整个音节。不过，不是任意的声母和韵母都可组成有意义的音节，就是说，有的组合在汉语里是不存在的。以我们已学过的声母和单韵母为例，可组成以下音节。

【Illustration 1】

The basic structure of a syllable in *pinyin* is: Initial + Final; the entire syllable is permeated with a tone. But not any combination of initials and finals can make up syllables which have meanings, i.e. some syllables do not exist. Take the initials and finals we have learned as examples, they can make up of the following syllables.

	b	p	m	f	d	t	n	l	g	k	h
a	ba	pa	ma	fa	da	ta	na	la	ga	ka	ha
o	bo	po	mo	fo				lo			
e			me		de	te	ne	le	ge	ke	he
i	bi	pi	mi		di	ti	ni	li			
u	bu	pu	mu	fu	du	tu	nu	lu	gu	ku	hu
ü							nü	lü			

 说明 2

声调贯穿于音节的整个发音过程中。不过，并不是每个音节都有第一声、第二声、第三声、第四声这四个声调。

【Illustration 2】
Tones penetrate into the whole pronunciation of initials and finals. Not all syllables will have the four tones, i.e. first tone, second tone, third tone and fourth tone.

hē
喝（drink）

hé
河（river）

hè
鹤（crane）

声母与单韵母的拼读
(Spelling and Pronunciation of Initials and Simple Finals)

b、p、m、f 的拼读 (Spelling and pronunciation of "b, p, m, f")

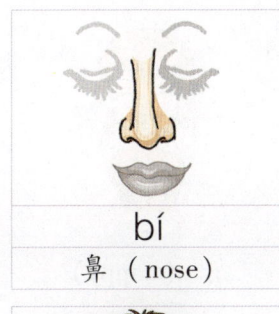
bí
鼻（nose）

bǐ
笔（pencil）

bì
币（coin）

bù
不（no）

pà
怕（afraid）

pò
破（worn out）

13

mǎ
马 (horse)

mō
摸 (touch)

fó
佛 (Buddha)

d、t、n、l 的拼读 (Spelling and pronunciation of "d, t, n, l")

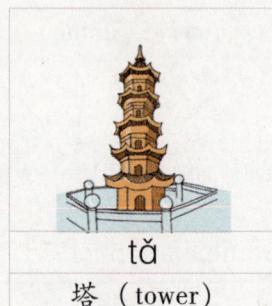
tǎ
塔 (tower)

dù
肚 (belly)

tù
兔 (rabbit)

tī
梯 (ladder)

nǔ
女 (female)

lè
乐 (happy)

lí
梨 (pear)

lù
路 (road)

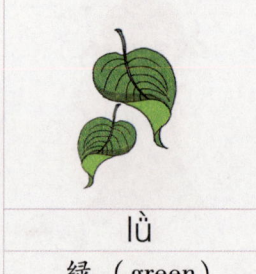
lǜ
绿 (green)

g、k、h 的拼读（Spelling and pronunciation of "g, k, h"）

gǔ
鼓（drum）

kǎ
卡（card）

kū
哭（cry）

hā
哈（ha ha）

hē
喝（drink）

hǔ
虎（tiger）

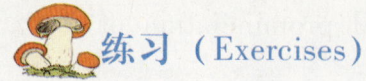
练习（Exercises）

一、听录音，跟读，注意每组声母的区别：

Listen to the tape and repeat what you hear. Pay attention to the differences between each group of initials.

| 1. | b | p | | 2. | d | t | | 3. | g | k | | 4. | m | n |
| 5. | h | f | | 6. | b | d | | 7. | t | f | | 8. | h | n |

二、听录音，把下面的声母按听到的顺序写在空格里：

Listen to the tape and write down the initials you hear in the following blanks.

b　p　m　f　d　t　n　l　g　k　h

| 1. | 2. | 3. | 4. | 5. | 6. |
| 7. | 8. | 9. | 10. | 11. | |

三、听录音，给下面的拼音加上声调：

Listen to the tape and give the *pinyin* tone-marks.

| bo | ge | nu | he | ma | lü | li | mo |
| ka | le | pa | nü | mo | lu | fa | fo |

四、听录音，在与听到的拼音一致的答案后面画√：

Listen to the tape and mark "√" after the *pinyin* you have heard.

1.	bó	pó		6.	lú	lǘ
2.	mǔ	mǒ		7.	hā	fā
3.	lè	là		8.	nǐ	lǐ
4.	pā	bā		9.	bì	dì
5.	kè	gè		10.	nǚ	nǔ

五、听录音，按所听到的词语的顺序在图的下面写上序号：

Listen to the tape and number the following pictures according to the sequence that you hear them on the tape.

（一）1~4

pà　（　　）　mǎ　（　　）　tǎ　（　　）　kǎ　（　　）

（二）5~8

tī　（　　）　bì　（　　）　lí　（　　）　bí　（　　）

（三）9~12

tù　（　　）　dù　（　　）　lǜ　（　　）　nǚ　（　　）

第二课　声母（一）

六、朗读下面的拼音，体会每组拼音的区别：

Read aloud the following *pinyin* and try to distinguish the differences between each group of syllables.

gǔ	kǔ	dí	tí
骨	苦	笛	蹄
bone	bitter	flute	hoof

dā	tā	tǔ	dǔ
搭	塌	吐	赌
set up	collapse	spit	gamble

ní	lí	fǔ	hǔ
泥	梨	斧	虎
mud	pear	axe	tiger

七、朗读下面的拼音：

Read aloud the following *pinyin*.

bǐyù	pífū	mǎlù	míyǔ
比喻	皮肤	马路	谜语
analogy	skin	road	riddle

mùdì	mìmì	fǎlǜ	fúwù
目的	秘密	法律	服务
purpose	secret	law	service

18

fùnǚ	dǔbó	tǐyù	nǔlì
妇女	赌博	体育	努力
woman	gamble	physical exercise	effort

lǐwù	lǐ fà	gēwǔ	kělè
礼物	理发	歌舞	可乐
gift	have a haircut	singing and dancing	cola

八、用连线的方法将下面的图与相应的拼音连接在一起：

Match the picture to the corresponding *pinyin*.

mǎ

nǚ

bǐ

hè

pò

lù

九、按照顺序将学过的单韵母和声母默写一遍：

From memory, write down the simple finals and initials you have learnt auording to the order.

单韵母

声母

第三课 复韵母(一)

Lesson Three Compound Finals (I)

以 a、o、e 开头的复韵母
(Compound Finals that Begin with "a"," o"or"e")

说明 1

汉语拼音中以 a、o、e 开头的复韵母共有 4 个。

【Illustration 1】

There are four compound finals that begin with the simple finals "a", "o" or "e" in *pinyin*.

ai　　ei　　ao　　ou

说明 2

以上四个复韵母分别由两个单元音组成,发音时从前一个单元音向后一个单元音过渡。

【Illustration 2】

The above four compound finals consist of two simple finals. When pronouncing them, it is imperative to have a natural glide but not a sudden change from the first final to the second final.

a + i ⇨ ai
e + i ⇨ ei
a + o ⇨ ao

（这里 o 的发音接近于 u）

(Here, the sound "o" is similar to that of "u".)

$$o + u \Rightarrow ou$$

（这里 o 的发音接近于 e）

(Here, the sound "o" is similar to that of "e".)

说明 3

ai、ei、ao、ou 可以作为单独的音节使用。

【Illustration 3】

"ai", "ei", "ao" or "ou" can be individual syllables.

ài

爱（love）

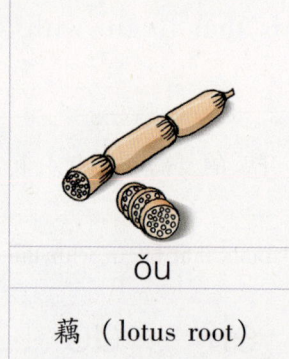

ǒu

藕（lotus root）

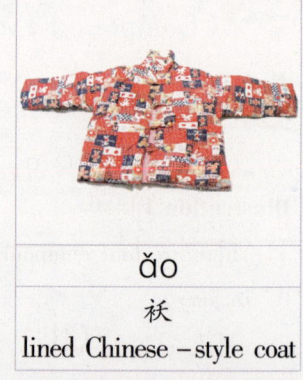

ǎo

袄
lined Chinese-style coat

以 i 开头的复韵母 (Compound Finals that Begin with "i")

说明 1

汉语拼音中以 i 开头的复韵母共有 4 个。

【Illustration 1】

There are four compound finals that begin with "i" in *Pinyin*.

$$ia \quad ie \quad iao \quad iou$$

说明 2

以上四个复韵母分别由二至三个单元音组成。发音时从前面的单元音向后面的单元音过渡。

【Illustration 2】
　　The above four compound finals consist of two or three simple finals. When pronouncing them, it is imperative to have a natural glide but not a sudden change from the beginning to the end of the compound final.

$$i + a \Rightarrow ia$$
$$i + e \Rightarrow ie$$

（这里的 e 开口度要大一些）
(Here, the sound "e" is more open.)

$$i + (a + o) \Rightarrow iao$$

（这里的 o 接近于 u）
(Here, the sound "o" is similar to that of "u".)

$$i + (o + u) \Rightarrow iou$$

（这里的 o 接近于 e）
(The sound "o" here is similar to that of "e")

说明 3

　　以 i 开头的复韵母作为独立音节使用时，i 变成 y。ia、ie、iou、iao 要写成 ya、ye、you、yao。

【Illustration 3】
　　When compound finals that begin with "i" are used as individual syllables, the "i" changes to "y". Examples: "ia, ie, iou, iao" change to "ya, ye, you, yao".

yā

鸭（duck）

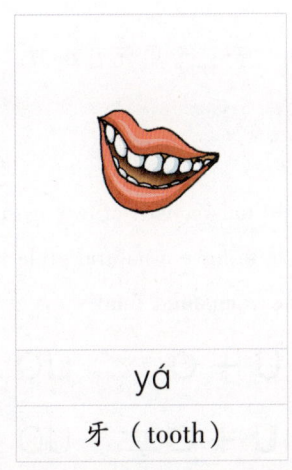

yá

牙（tooth）

yè

夜（night）

yóu	yǎo	yào
油（oil）	咬（bite）	药（drug）

以 u 开头的复韵母 (Compound Finals that Begin with "u")

🌵 说明 1

汉语拼音中以 u 开头的复韵母共有 4 个。

【Illustration 1】

There are four compound finals that begin with "u" in *Pinyin*.

ua   uo   uai   uei

🌵 说明 2

以上四个复韵母分别由二至三个单元音组成。发音时从前面的单元音向后面的单元音过渡。

【Illustration 2】

The above four compound finals consist of two or three simple finals. When pronouncing them, it is imperative to have a natural glide but not a sudden change from the beginning to the end of the compound final.

u + a ⇨ ua

u + o ⇨ uo

（这里的 o 接近于 e）

(Here, the sound "o" is similar to that of "e".)

$$u + (a+i) \Rightarrow uai$$
$$u + (e+i) \Rightarrow uei$$

说明 3

以 u 开头的复韵母作为独立音节使用时，u 变成 w。ua、uo、uai、uei 要写成 wa、wo、wai、wei。

【Illustration 3】

When compound finals that begin with "u" are used as individual syllables, "u" changes into "w". Examples: "ua, uo, uai, uei" change to "wa, wo, wai, wei".

wā

挖（dig）

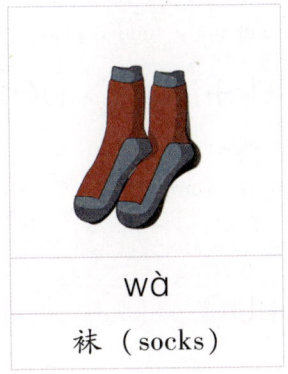

wà

袜（socks）

wō

窝（nest）

wò

握（shake hands）

wāi

歪（askew）

wèi

喂（feed）

以 ü 开头的复韵母 (Compound Finals that Begin with "ü")

说明 1

汉语拼音中以 ü 开头的复韵母只有 1 个。

【Illustration 1】

There is only one compound final that begins with "ü" in *Pinyin*.

üe

说明 2

üe 是由 ü 和 e 组成的。发音时从 ü 向 e 过渡。

【Illustration 2】

"üe" consists of "ü" and "e". When pronouncing this compound final, it is imperative to have a natural glide but not a sudden change from "ü" to "e".

ü + e ⇒ üe

（这里的 e 开口度要大一些）

(Here, when pronouncing the sound "e", the mouth has to open wider)

说明 3

以 ü 开头的复韵母作为独立音节出现时，要去掉 ü 上边的两个点，在前边加上 y，变成 yue。

【Illustration 3】

When compound finals that begin with "ü" appear as individual syllables, the two dots above "ü" shall be omitted and the letter "y" is placed before the "u". Example："yue".

yuè

月 （moon）

复韵母的拼写规则 (Spelling Rules of Compound Finals)

说明 1

iou 和 uei 与声母拼写时，中间的 o 和 e 省略不写。如：声母 d 和韵母 iou 拼写成 diu；声母 g 和韵母 uei 拼写成 gui。

【Illustration 1】

When "iou" or "uei" are spelled with initials, the letters "o" or "e" shall be omitted.

Examples："d" + "iou" → "diu"; "g" + "uei" → "gui".

说明 2

【Illustration 2】

复韵母的声调标法（Tones of Compound Finals）：

1. 当复韵母中有 a 的时候，无论 a 在前在后，声调都要标在 a 的上面。如 guā、lái、biǎo 等等。

    In syllables having a compound final with an "a", a tone mark shall be placed above the "a" no matter where the "a" is located. Examples: guā, lái, biǎo.

2. 当复韵母中没有 a 而有 e 或 o 的时候，无论其在前在后，声调都要标在 e 或 o 的上面。（e 和 o 不会在同一音节中出现）。如：guó、lèi、yuè、gǒu 等等。

    In syllables having a compound final with an "e" or "o" but no "a", no matter where the "e" or "o" is located, a tone mark shall be marked placed above the "e" or "o". (Note: "e" and "o" will not appear in the same syllable). Examples: "guó", "lèi", "yuè", "gǒu".

3. iou 和 uei 前边有声母时，中间的 o 和 e 被省略了，因此，本应该标在 o 和 e 上的声调顺延，标在后面的 u 和 i 上。如：diū、guì 等等。

    When "iou" and "uei" are spelled with initials, the letters "o" or "e" shall be omitted. Therefore tones that were marked above "o" or "e" shall be marked above the "u" or "i".

    Examples: "diū", "guì" etc.

声母（一）与复韵母拼合表
(Table of Combinations of Initials (I) and Compound Finals)

	b	p	m	f	d	t	n	l	g	k	h
ai	bai	pai	mai		dai	tai	nai	lai	gai	kai	hai
ei	bei	pei	mei	fei	dei	tei	nei	lei	gei	kei	hei
ao	bao	pao	mao		dao	tao	nao	lao	gao	kao	hao
ou		pou	mou	fou	dou	tou	nou	lou	gou	kou	hou
ia					dia			lia			
ie	bie	pie	mie		die	tie	nie	lie			
iao	biao	piao	miao		diao	tiao	niao	liao			
iou			miu		diu		niu	liu			
ua									gua	kua	hua
uo					duo	tuo	nuo	luo	guo	kuo	huo
uai									guai	kuai	huai
uei					dui	tui			gui	kui	hui
üe							nüe	lüe			

声母（一）与复韵母的拼读
(Spelling and Pronunciation of Initials (I) and Compound Finals)

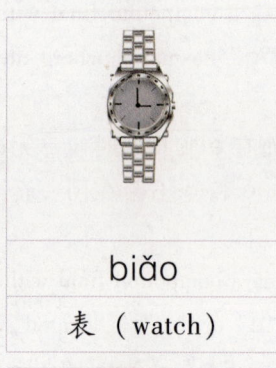

biě
瘪（flat）

biǎo
表（watch）

māo
猫（cat）

pái
牌（cards）

pǎo
跑（run）

niǎo
鸟（bird）

趣味汉语拼音课本（基础篇）

fēi	dāo	gǒu
飞（fly）	刀（knife）	狗（dog）
niú	lóu	hóu
牛（cattle）	楼（building）	猴（monkey）
guī	hǎi	huā
龟（turtle）	海（sea）	花（flower）

第三课 复韵母（一）

练习（Exercises）

一、听录音，按所听到的顺序在相应的复韵母的下面写上序号：

Listen to the tape and number the following compound finals according to the sequence you hear them.

ai	ei	ao	ou	ia	ie	iao	iou	ua	uo	uai	uei	üe

二、听录音，给下面的拼音加上声调：

Listen to the tape and place the appropriate tone marks on the *pinyin*.

1. lai	2. lüe	3. wei	4. kuai	5. liu	6. gua
7. ye	8. lao	9. liao	10. ya	11. lie	12. gui
13. yao	14. hei	15. hui	16. wai	17. you	18. wo

三、听录音，在与听到的拼音一致的答案后面画√：

Listen to the tape and write "√" after the *pinyin* you hear.

1.	dōu	duō	6.	nüè	niè
2.	niú	liú	7.	huī	hēi
3.	diǎ	dǎi	8.	bǎo	biǎo
4.	lèi	liè	9.	biè	bèi
5.	kuā	kā	10.	guài	gài

四、听录音，将下列拼音中缺少的复韵母补上并加上声调：

Listen to the tape and fill in the blanks with the compound finals and tones you hear.

1. d	2. f	3. k	4. n	5. l
6. p	7. m	8. t	9. g	10. b

五、比较下面的拼音，在标错声调的拼音右边画 ×：

Compare the following *pinyin* and decide whether the tones' positions are correct or incorrect; write "×" if it is incorrect.

1	gǎi	gaǐ		6	mào	maò
2	huaì	huài		7	weì	wèi
3	kuì	kùi		8	mìao	miào
4	kūa	kuā		9	leì	lèi
5	liù	lìu		10	liǎ	lǐa

六、将下面的声母与可以搭配的复韵母拼写在一起，填写在下面的表格中：

Match each initial to the corresponding compound final. Write down the answers in the following forms.

声母	复韵母
b	ai
	ei
	ao
	ou
t	ia
	ie
	iao
	iou
n	ua
	uo
	uai
g	uei
	üe

b + 复韵母

| | | | | | | |

t + 复韵母

| | | | | | | |

n + 复韵母

| | | | | | | |

g + 复韵母

| | | | | | | |

七、朗读下面的拼音，体会每组拼音的区别：

Read aloud the following *pinyin* and try to distinguish the differences between each group of syllables.

fá	huá	pào	bào
罚	滑	炮	报
punish	slip	cannon	newspaper

duō	tuō	diào	tiào
多	脱	钓	跳
many	take off	fishing	jump

八、朗读下面的拼音：

Read aloud the following *pinyin*.

báicài	mǎimài	niúnǎi	guòlái
白菜	买卖	牛奶	过来
Chinese cabbage	buying and selling	milk	come here

měihuà	láolèi	hēibái	bāoguǒ
美化	劳累	黑白	包裹
beautify	tired	black and white	package

gāolóu	hòulái	tiàogāo	huí guó
高楼	后来	跳高	回国
tall buildings	later	high jump	return to one´s country

huáibào	tuífèi	guīhuà	nüèdài
怀抱	颓废	规划	虐待
embrace	dispirited	program	ill-treat

九、看图，在图下面的空格里写出相应的拼音：

Look at the pictures and write down the corresponding pinyin in each blank underneath the pictures.

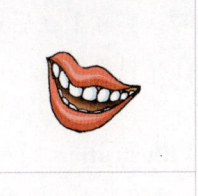

第四课　声母（二）

Lesson Four　Initials（Ⅱ）

舌尖声母（二）Apical Sound in Initials（Ⅱ）

说明 1

汉语拼音的舌尖声母共有 7 个。我们在第二课已经学习了 d、t、n、l，在这一课，我们学习另外的 3 个。

【Illustration 1】

There are 7 apical sounds in initials in pinyin. We learned 4 of them（d, t, n, l）in Lesson Two. Here, we will learn the other three.

z　c　s

说明 2

因为 z、c、s 是辅音，如果不加上元音很难发出，所以我们在发这些音时，实际上在后边加上了一个元音，写做 i。这个 i 不同于单韵母中的 i，它的存在只是使 z、c、s 在发音时舌尖能用上力，形成两个舌高点，一个在舌尖，一个在舌面后部，舌尖接近上齿背，但不发生摩擦，嘴唇不圆。

【Illustration 2】

Consonants "z", "c" and "s" are difficult to pronounce without adding a vowel, so we add the vowel "i" when pronouncing them. Here, the "i" is pronounced differently from the "i" in simple finals. It only follows the consonants "z", "c" or "s". When pronouncing these consonants, the tongue forms two high points, with one point-the front-slightly higher the other-the back. The tongue's tip lightly touches the hard palate near the upper teeth ridge for the front point, followed by a slight dip and then rise. The lips retract back reducing friction of air movement.

说明 3

zi、ci、si 为独立音节。

【Illustration 3】

"zi", "ci" or "si" as individual syllables.

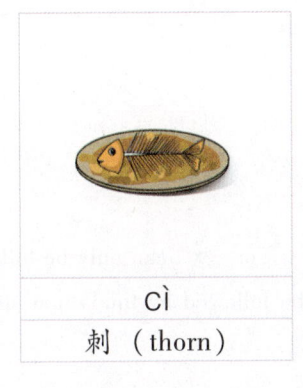

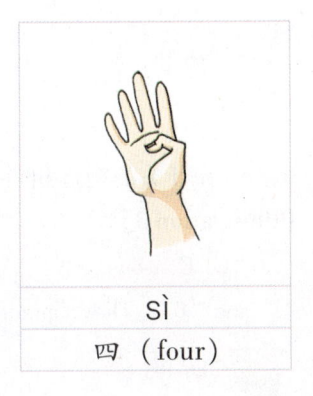

zì	cì	sì
字 (character)	刺 (thorn)	四 (four)

舌面声母 (Dorsal Sounds in Initials)

说明 1

汉语拼音的舌面声母共有 3 个。

【Illustration 1】

There are 3 dorsal sounds in initials in *pinyin*.

j q x

说明 2

因为 j、q、x 是辅音，如果不加上元音很难发出，所以我们在发这 3 个音时，实际上在后边加上了单韵母 i。

【Illustration 2】

The Consonants "j, q, x" are difficult to pronounce without adding a vowel, so we add the simple final "i" when pronouncing them.

jī	qī	xǐ
鸡（chick）	七（seven）	洗（wash）

🌵 说明 3

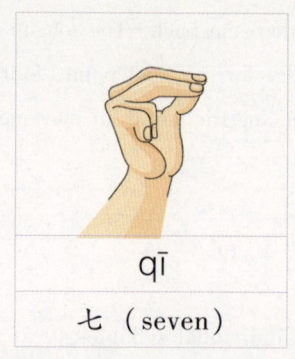

在汉语拼音音节中，j、q、x 只能与 i 和 ü 开头的韵母相拼，而不能与 a、o、e、u 开头的韵母相拼。

【Illustration 3】

The Consonants "j", "q" or "x" can only be followed by finals that start with "i" and "ü". They cannot be followed by finals that start with "a", "o", "e".

🌵 说明 4

j、q、x 这组声母在与 ü 开头的韵母相拼时，韵母 ü 上的两个点应该省略。如：q 和 ü 相拼，声调为第一声，汉语拼音写做 qū。

【Illustration 4】

When a final starts with "ü" and is preceded by "j", "q", "x", the two dots above "ü" shall be omitted.

jǔ	qǔ
举（lift）	曲（melody）

卷舌声母 (Retroflex Initials)

说明 1

汉语拼音的卷舌声母共有 4 个。

【Illustration 1】

There are 4 retroflex initials in *pinyin*.

zh　　ch　　sh　　r

说明 2

因为 zh、ch、sh、r 是辅音，如果不加上元音很难发出，所以我们在发这些音时，实际上在后边加上了一个元音，写做 i。这个 i 不同于单韵母的 i，也不同于 z、c、s 后边的 i，它与在 z、c、s 后边的 "i" 发音方法相同，但舌高点不同，舌尖接近硬腭，所形成的第一舌高点靠后，第二舌高点则靠前。

【Illustration 2】

The consonants "zh", "ch", "sh" and "r" are difficult to pronounce without adding a final, so we add the vowel "i" when pronouncing them. Here, "i" is pronounced differently from the "i" in the simple finals. It also differs from the "i" following the consonants "z", "c" or "s". The position of the high point of the tongue is curled towards the back part of the mouth obstructing the flow of air.

说明 3

zh、ch、sh、r 加 i 变成 zhi、chi、shi、ri 成为独立音节。

【Illustration 3】

We add "i" to "zh", "ch", "sh" or "r", then we get "zhi", "chi", "shi" or "ri" as individual syllables.

zhī	chī	shí	rì
织 (weave)	吃 (eat)	十 (ten)	日 (sun)

如何掌握以上三组声母的发音
(How to Pronounce the above Three Groups of Initials)

说明

这三组声母是汉语拼音中最难发的三组音,因此在发音时要特别注意它们的区别。相对来说,z 组声母比较容易,先掌握好它们的发音方法和发音部位,然后在此基础上变化发音部位就可以发出 zh 组和 j 组。下面以 z、zh、j 为例:

【Illustration】

The above three groups of initials are the most difficult pronunciations in *pinyin*. Comparing pronunciations, group "z" is easiest. We can grasp the pronunciations of groups "zh" and "j" on the basis of the manner and position of group "z" by changing the position of the tongue. Take "z", "zh" and "j" for example.

发音方法不变,舌尖卷起 (No change in manner of articulation except for curling the tip of the tongue towards the back of the mouth). → Zh

z

发音方法不变,发音部位略向后移,舌面略拱起 (No change in manner of articulation except for moving the position of the tongue backwards and arching the lingual surface, i.e. first placing the tip of the tongue against the lower teeth, curl the tongue back bringing its tip up to the hard palate which blocks the movement of air). → j

声母(二)与韵母拼合表
(Table of Combinations of Initials (Ⅱ) and Finals)

说明

z、c、s 和 zh、ch、sh、r 这两组声母与 j、q、x 在与韵母的配合关系上表现出很整齐的互补局面。z、c、s 和 zh、ch、sh、r 一般只与 a、o、e、u 开头的韵母相拼，不与 i、ü 开头的韵母相拼，而 j、q、x 则正好相反。

【Illustration】

Groups "z", "c", "s" and "zh", "ch", "sh", "r" are complementary to group "j, q, x" when matching with finals. The first two groups match to finals beginning with "a", "o", "e", or "u". Group "j, q, x" match to finals beginning with "i" or "ü".

	z	c	s	zh	ch	sh	r	j	q	x
a	za	ca	sa	zha	cha	sha				
o										
e	ze	ce	se	zhe	che	she	re			
i								ji	qi	xi
u	zu	cu	su	zhu	chu	shu	ru			
ü								jü	qü	xü
ai	zai	cai	sai	zhai	chai	shai				
ei	zei	cei		zhei		shei				
ao	zao	cao	sao	zhao	chao	shao	rao			
ou	zou	cou	sou	zhou	chou	shou	rou			
ia								jia	qia	xia
ie								jie	qie	xie
iao								jiao	qiao	xiao
iou								jiu	qiu	xiu
ua				zhua	chua	shua	rua			
uo	zuo	cuo	suo	zhuo	chuo	shuo	ruo			
uai				zhuai	chuai	shuai				
uei	zui	cui	sui	zhui	chui	shui	rui			
üe								jue	que	xue

声母（二）与韵母的拼读
（Spelling and Pronunciation of Initials (Ⅱ) and Finals）

z、c、s 的拼读（Spelling and pronunciation of "z", "c" and "s"）

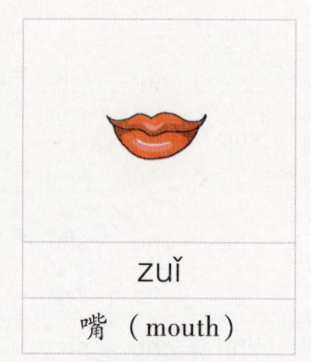

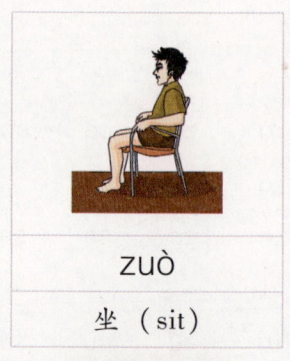

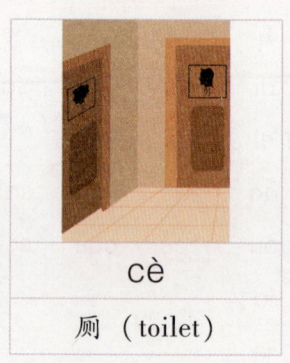

zǒu	zuǐ	zuò
走（walk）	嘴（mouth）	坐（sit）

cā	cài	cè
擦（wipe）	菜（vegetable）	厕（toilet）

sǎo	sài	suǒ
扫（sweep）	赛（race）	锁（lock）

j、q、x 的拼读（Spelling and pronunciation of "j", "q" and "x"）

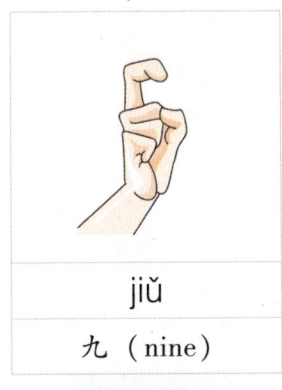

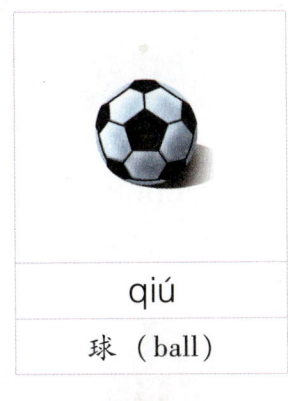

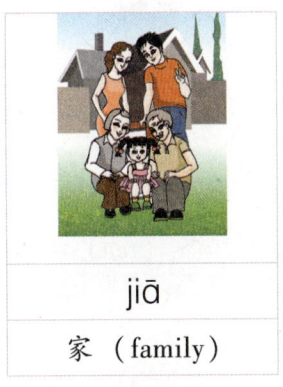

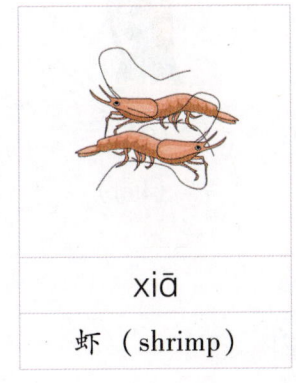

jiǔ	qiú	jiā
九（nine）	球（ball）	家（family）

xuě	xiā	xué
雪（snow）	虾（shrimp）	学（study）

zh、ch、sh、r 的拼读（Spelling and pronunciation of "zh", "ch", "sh" and "r"）

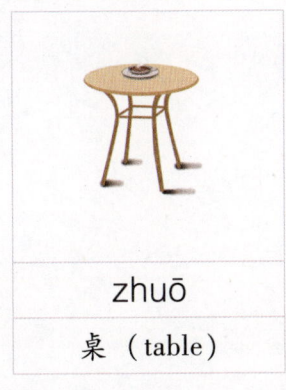

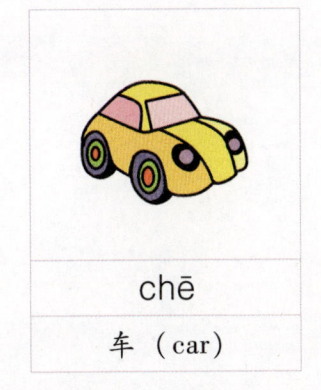

zhū	zhuō	chē
猪（pig）	桌（table）	车（car）

第四课 声母（二）

chá	chuī	shū
茶 (tea)	吹 (blow)	书 (book)

shǒu	rè	ròu
手 (hand)	热 (hot)	肉 (meat)

练习 (Exercises)

一、听写声母，将听到的声母按顺序写在下面的空格里：

Listen to the tape and write down the initials you hear, in order, in the following blanks.

1.	2.	3.	4.	5.	6.	7.	8.	9.	10.

二、听录音，在与听到的拼音一致的答案后面画√：

Listen to the tape and write "√" after the *pinyin* you hear.

1.	chā	qiā	6.	qué	qié
2.	zāi	zhāi	7.	ròu	ruò
3.	jiǔ	zhǒu	8.	rè	rù
4.	jiǎo	qiǎo	9.	shǒu	sǒu
5.	cuī	suī	10.	sì	sù

三、听录音，将下列拼音中缺少的声母补上：

Listen to the tape and fill in the blanks with the initials you hear.

1. __uā	2. __ài	3. __iǔ	4. __òu	5. __uē
6. __ǎo	7. __iā	8. __éi	9. __uò	10. __uì

四、听两遍录音，根据听到的音节选择下面的声母和韵母，把它们拼写在一起，并加上声调：

Listen to the tape twice and write down the syllables you hear by combining the given initials, finals, and tones.

z	c	s	j	q	x	zh	ch	sh	r
üe	ie	uai	ou	ia	ai	uo	uei	ei	ao

五、改正下面拼音中的错误，将正确的拼音写在错误拼音的右边：

Correct the errors in *pinyin* and write down the correct answers to the right of each one.

1.	qüē	2.	jiǒu	3.	yüè	4.	yiě
5.	luè	6.	kuèi	7.	uǒ	8.	yǔ

六、将下面的声母与可以搭配的复韵母拼写在一起，填写在下面的表格中：

Match each initial to the corresponding compound final and write down the answers in the following forms.

声母

sh
z
r
q

复韵母

ai
ao
ei
ou
ia
ie
iao
iou
ua
uo
uai
uei
üe

sh + 复韵母

z + 复韵母

r + 复韵母

q + 复韵母

七、朗读下面的拼音：

Read aloud the following *pinyin*.

zázhì	shòu zuì	cèsuǒ	cǎisè
杂志	受罪	厕所	彩色
magazine	endure hardships	toilet	multicolor

sǎochú	sōusuǒ	zuòzhě	zhùzhái
扫除	搜索	作者	住宅
clean up	search	author	residence

chájù	chūjí	shèjì	shùxué
茶具	初级	设计	数学
tea set	primary	design	maths

rè shuǐ	rújiā	jīqì	jiàzhào
热水	儒家	机器	驾照
hot water	Confucianism	machine	driver license

qǐshì	quēxí	xiǎochī	xuéxí
启事	缺席	小吃	学习
notice	absent	snack	study

八、朗读下面的拼音，注意声母之间的区别：

Read aloud the following *pinyin*. Try to distinguish the differences of initials in each group.

zǎocāo	zūzhù	shòuròu
早操	租住	瘦肉
morning exercises	rent rooms	lean meat

xiéjiē	xiǎoqiǎo	zhuīsuí
斜街	小巧	追随
(oblique street)	small and exquisite	follow

九、看图，在图下面的空格里写出相应的拼音：

Look at the pictures and write down the corresponding *pinyin* in the blanks under the pictures.

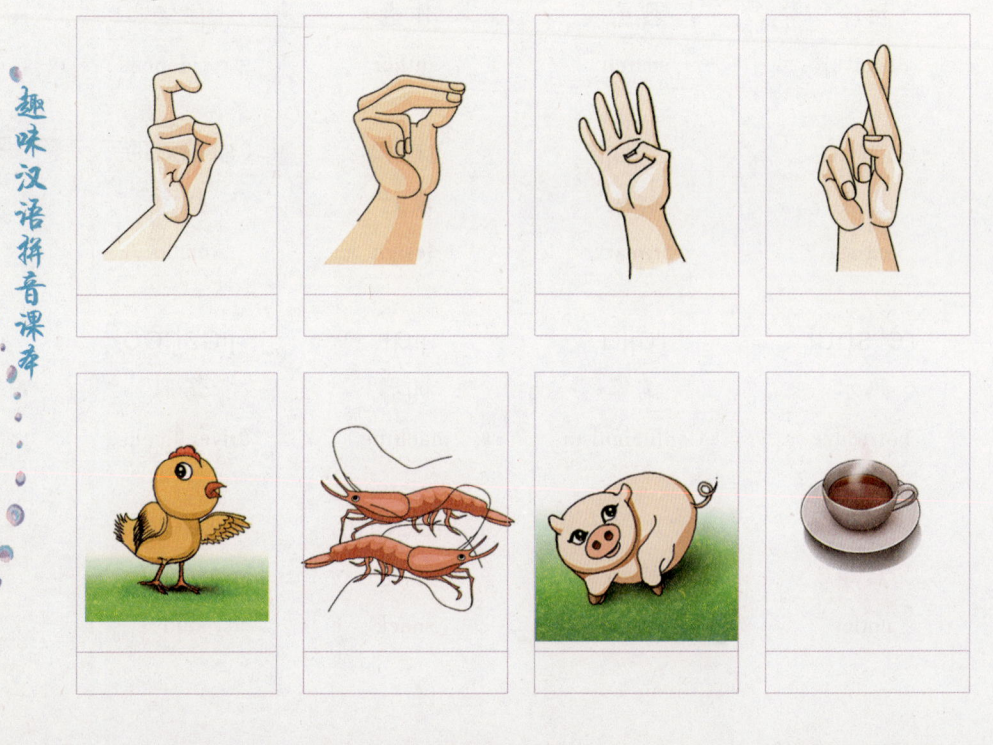

十、朗读下面的绕口令：

Read aloud the following tongue twisters.

Sì shì sì,

四 是 四, Four is four

shí shì shí.

十 是 十。Ten is ten

shísì shì shísì,

十四 是 十四, Fourteen is fourteen

Sìshí shì sìshí.

四十 是 四十。Forty is forty

第五课 复韵母（二）

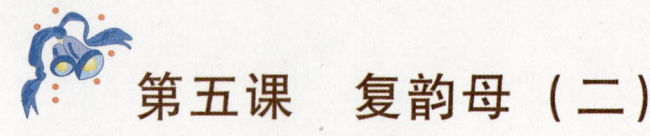

Lesson Five Compound Finals (II)

前鼻音韵母 (Front Nasal Sound in Compound Finals)

说明 1

汉语拼音中的前鼻音韵母共有 8 个。

【Illustration 1】

There are 8 front nasal compound finals in *pinyin*.

an　　en　　ian　　in

uan　　uen　　üan　　ün

说明 2

对于一些初学者来说，前鼻音韵母比较难发，其主要原因是找不到 n 的发音部位。这里介绍一种"倒读法"。以 an 为例，先慢慢发出 n 和 a，拼读出 na，然后迅速闭上嘴发出 a 和 n，就会很容易地拼读出 an。

【Illustration 2】

It is difficult for the beginners to pronounce the front nasal compound finals mainly because they cannot articulate the "n". I will introduce a "Backward Reading Manner" method. Example: If you want to pronounce "an", please pronounce "n" and "a" slowly – "na", and then close your mouth quickly while pronouncing "a" and "n" — "an". See the picture.

n ⇆ a

说明 3

【Illustration 3】

1. in 作为独立音节出现时，要在前面加上 y，变成 yin。

If "in" is used as an individual syllable, "y" is placed in front of it.

Example："in" → "yin".

2. "uen" 前边出现声母时，韵母 e 省略，声调标在 u 上。如：dūn 就是由 d 和 uen 再加上声调组成的。

The final "e" shall be omitted when there is an initial in front of the compound final "uen". The tone shall be marked above the "u".

Example："d" + "uen" ("the first tone") → "dūn".

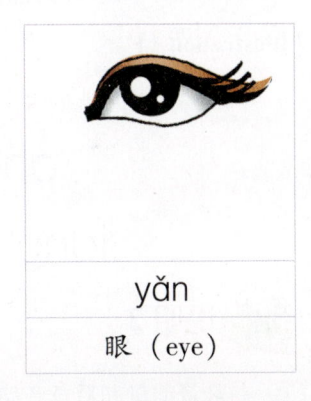

àn	yān	yǎn
按（press）	烟（cigarette）	眼（eye）
yìn	wǎn	wěn
印（seal）	碗（bowl）	吻（kiss）

第五课　复韵母（二）

wèn	yún	yuán
问 (ask)	云 (cloud)	圆 (round)

后鼻音韵母 (Back Nasal Compound Finals)

说明 1

汉语拼音中的后鼻音韵母共有 8 个。

【Illustration 1】

There are 8 back nasal compound finals in *Pinyin*.

$$\text{ang} \quad \text{eng} \quad \text{ong} \quad \text{ing}$$
$$\text{iang} \quad \text{iong} \quad \text{uang} \quad \text{ueng}$$

说明 2

前鼻音韵母和后鼻音韵母的韵尾从口型上看有很大的不同。

【Illustration 2】

There are big differences in the shape of the mouth between the front and the back nasal compound finals when pronouncing them.

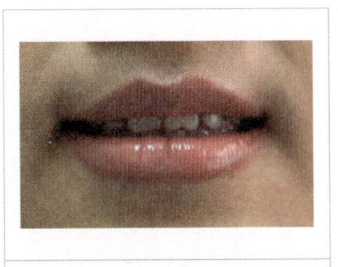

an 的正面口型

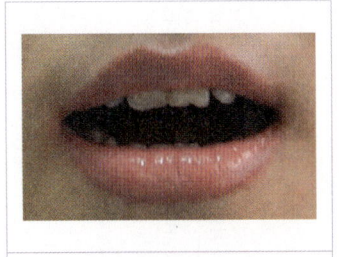

ang 的正面口型

说明 3
【Illustration 3】

1. ing 作为独立音节出现时，要在前面加上 y，变成 ying。
   If "ing" is used as an individual syllable, "y" is placed in front of it. Example："ing" → "ying".
2. ong 不能作为独立音节出现。
   "ong" cannot be an individual syllable.
3. ueng 只能作为独立音节出现。
   "ueng" can only be an individual syllable.

áng
昂（hold one's head high）

yīng
鹰（eagle）

yáng
羊（sheep）

yǒng
泳（swim）

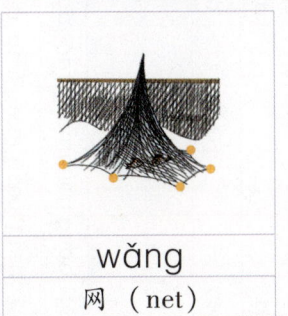

wǎng
网（net）

wēng
翁（old man）

第五课　复韵母（二）

声母与鼻韵母拼合表 (Table of Combinations of Initials and Nasal Compound Finals)

	b	p	m	f	d	t	n	l	g	k	h	j	q	x	z	c	s	zh	ch	sh	r
an	ban	pan	man	fan	dan	tan	nan	lan	gan	kan	han				zan	can	san	zhan	chan	shan	ran
en	ben	pen	men	fen	den		nen		gen	ken	hen				zen	cen	sen	zhen	chen	shen	ren
ian	bian	pian	mian		dian	tian	nian	lian				jian	qian	xian							
in	bin	pin	min				nin	lin				jin	qin	xin							
uan					duan	tuan	nuan	luan	guan	kuan	huan				zuan	cuan	suan	zhuan	chuan	shuan	ruan
uen					dun	tun		lun	gun	kun	hun				zun	cun	sun	zhun	chun	shun	run
üan												juan	quan	xuan							
ün												jun	qun	xun							
ang	bang	pang	mang	fang	dang	tang	nang	lang	gang	kang	hang				zang	cang	sang	zhang	chang	shang	rang
eng	beng	peng	meng	feng	deng	teng	neng	leng	geng	keng	heng				zeng	ceng	seng	zheng	cheng	sheng	reng
ong					dong	tong	nong	long	gong	kong	hong				zong	cong	song	zhong	chong		rong
iang							niang	liang				jiang	qiang	xiang							
ing	bing	ping	ming		ding	ting	ning	ling				jing	qing	xing							
iong												jiong	qiong	xiong							
uang									guang	kuang	huang							zhuang	chuang	shuang	
ueng																					

声母与复韵母（二）的拼读
（Spelling and Pronunciation of Initial and Compound Finals (Ⅱ)）

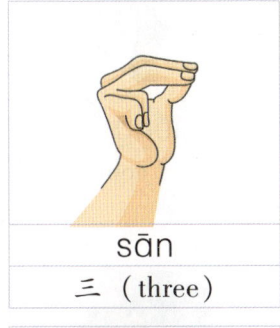

前鼻音韵母的拼读（Spelling and pronunciation of the front nasal finals.）

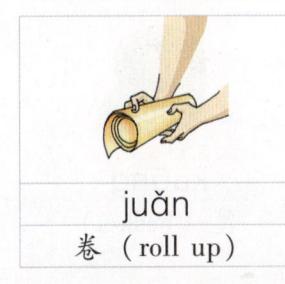

sān	shān	mén
三（three）	山（mountain）	门（door）

zhěn	qián	 tiān
枕（pillow）	钱（money）	天（sky）

lín	xìn	chuān
林（woods）	信（letter）	穿（to put on）

dūn	juǎn	qún
蹲(squat on the heels)	卷（roll up）	裙（skirt）

第五课　复韵母（二）

后鼻音韵母的拼读 (Spelling and pronunciation of the back nasal finals.)

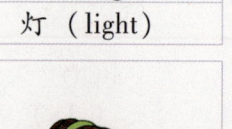

fáng	táng	lěng
房 (house)	糖 (candy)	冷 (cold)
dēng	lóng	sōng
灯 (light)	龙 (dragon)	松 (pine)
xiǎng	tīng	xīng
想 (think)	听 (listen)	星 (star)
xióng	kuāng	chuáng
熊 (bear)	筐 (basket)	床 (bed)

趣味汉语拼音课本 (基础篇)

练习（Exercises）

一、听写韵母，将听到的韵母按顺序写在下面的空格里：

Listen to the tape and write down the finals you hear, in order, in the following blanks.

1.	2.	3.	4.	5.	6.	7.	8.

9.	10.	11.	12.	13.	14.	15.	16.

二、听录音，在与听到的拼音一致的答案后面画√：

Listen to the tape and write "√" after the *pinyin* you have heard.

1.	chán	cháng
2.	liǎng	liǎn
3.	wàn	wàng
4.	yǔn	yǒng
5.	hóng	héng

6.	lín	líng
7.	jǐng	jiǒng
8.	kùn	kòng
9.	yuān	yān
10.	wēn	wēng

三、听录音，给下面的拼音加上声调：

Listen to the tape and add the tones you hear.

1.	lian	2.	yuan	3.	qiang	4.	kuang	5.	xiong
6.	lin	7.	kuan	8.	yun	9.	zhuan	10.	luan

四、听两遍录音，给下面由汉字组成的句子加上拼音：

Listen to the tape twice and write out the *pinyin* of the given characters in the sentences.

初	次	见	面	，	请	多	关	照	。

第五课 复韵母（二）

五、将下面表格中的声母和韵母拼合在一起，并加上相应的声调拼合，组成完整的拼音：

Write down the complete *pinyin* using the given initials, finals and tones.

1.	zh	uo	´
2.	l	üe	`
3.	h	uen	´
4.	ch	ou	ˇ
5.	n	ü	ˇ

6.	j	iou	-
7.	q	üan	´
8.	z	uei	`
9.	f	ei	ˇ
10.	b	iao	-

六、用连线的方法将下面的图和相应的拼音连接在一起：

Match the pictures to the corresponding *pinyin*.

chuān

qún

yǎn

lóng

wǎn

xióng

yáng

táng

七、朗读下面的拼音：

Read aloud the following *pinyin*.

cānguān	shēngchǎn	míngshān	shǎndiàn
参观	生产	名山	闪电
visit	produce	famous mountains	lightning

chéngmén	liángshuǎng	zhēnzhèng	diànyǐng
城门	凉爽	真正	电影
city gate	cool	ture	movie

zēngtiān	xīnnián	liànrén	jīnqián
增添	新年	恋人	金钱
add	new year	lover	money

pīngpāng	pīnyīn	hánlěng	sēnlín
乒乓	拼音	寒冷	森林
pingpong	*pinyin*	cold	forest

gāngqín	duànliàn	wēnnuǎn	liánhuān
钢琴	锻炼	温暖	联欢
piano	exercise	warm	have a get-together

guānkàn	zūnjìng	chūntiān	quánmiàn
观看	尊敬	春天	全面
watch	respect	spring	overall

xuānchuán	fǎngwèn	dāngxīn	jiànkāng
宣传	访问	当心	健康
propagandize	visit	Be careful	health

fēngkuáng	téngtòng	guāngróng	pínqióng
疯狂	疼痛	光荣	贫穷
crazy	ache	glory	poor

第五课 复韵母（二）

八、朗读下面的拼音，体会每组拼音声调的区别：

Read aloud the following *pinyin* and try to distinguish the differences between each group of tones.

fǎngwèn	fǎnwèn	zhǎnxīn	zhǎngxīn
访问	反问	崭新	掌心
visit	ask in reply	brand-new	the center of the palm

jiānnán	jiāngnán	qiánbì	qiángbì
艰难	江南	钱币	墙壁
hard	south of the Yangtze River	money	wall

rénmín	rénmíng	shàng chuán	shàng chuáng
人民	人名	上船	上床
people	name of a person	get on a boat	go to bed

九、将下面表格中缺少的韵母填上：

Fill in the blanks with the missing finals.

a		e	i	u	ü
ai	ei	ao			
ua	ie		iao		
ua	uo	uai			
üe					
an	en	ian	uan	uen	üan

| ang | eng | ong | ing | iang | | uang | ueng |

十、朗读下面的绕口令，注意前鼻音韵母和后鼻音韵母的区别：

Read aloud the following tongue twisters and pay attention to the differences between the front and back nasal finals.

Fěnhóng qiáng shàng huà fènghuáng,
粉红 墙 上 画 凤凰，Draw a phoenix on a pink wall

fènghuáng huà zài fěnhóng qiáng.
凤凰 画 在 粉红 墙。The phoenix is on the pink wall

Hóng fènghuáng,
红 凤凰，Red phoenix

fěn fènghuáng,
粉 凤凰，Pink phoenix

hóngfěn fènghuáng,
红粉 凤凰，Red pink phoenix

fěnhóng fènghuáng.
粉红 凤凰，Pink red phoenix

第五课 复韵母（二）

第六课　第三声的变调

Lesson Six　Third-tone Sandhi

第三声的变调（Third-tone Sandhi）

说明

第三声的字在单独念时，它的发音是固定的，可是在语流中，受后一音节声调的影响，会发生变化，我们称之为变调。

【Illustration】

The pronunciation of the syllable does not change when the third tone character appears independently. However, in the flow of speech with multiple syllables with third tones, it will change due to the effect of the following syllables. We call this change "Third Tone Sandhi".

第三声在非第三声音节前的变调

(Third-tone Sandhi is Used When a Third Tone is Followed by the Three Other Tones)

说明 1

在语流中，当前一个音节为第三声，后一个音节为第一声、第二声或第四声时，前一个第三声音节失去本调后边上升的部分，变为一个低降调。如下图所示：

【Illustration 1】

In the flow of speech, when the first syllable is in the third tone and the second syllable is in the first or second or fourth tone, the first syllable shall change the rising part of its tone to a low falling tone. See the picture.

变调前（before third-tone sandhi）　　变调后（after third-tone sandhi）

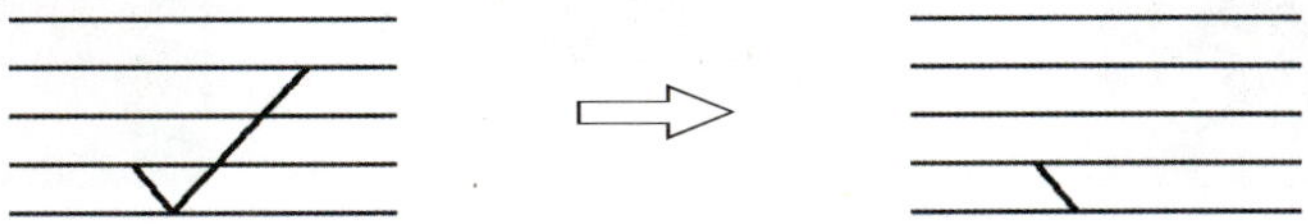

说明 2

三声变调只出现在发音的时候。书写的时候，还应该写成三声（ˇ）。

【Illustration 2】

Only when a syllable in the third-tone sandhi is read does it modify its tone. In writing it remains marked as the third tone.

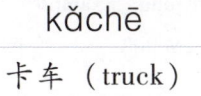

bǐnggān	kǎchē	hǎibiān
饼干（cookie）	卡车（truck）	海边（seaside）

cǎoméi	lǚyóu	zuǐchún
草莓（strawberry）	旅游（tour）	嘴唇（lips）

kǎoshì
考试（test）

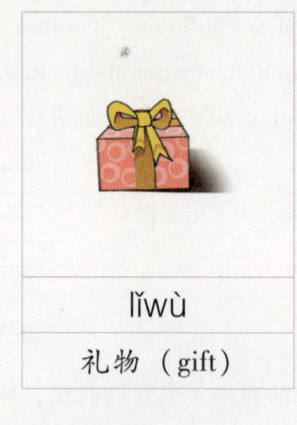

lǐwù
礼物（gift）

mǎlù
马路（road）

第三声在第三声音节前的变调
(Third-tone Sandhi in the Case of Two Third tones)

说明1

在语流中，当前一个音节为第三声，后一个音节也为第三声时，前一个第三声音节失去本调，读音近似于第二声。如下图所示：

【Illustration 1】

In the flow of speech, when two syllables are in the third tone, the first syllable shall change its tone to the second tone. Example：

变调前（before third-tone sandhi）　　变调后（after third-tone sandhi）

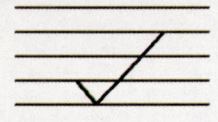

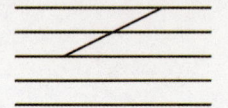

说明2

在书写时，前面的第三声音节仍标为第三声（ˇ），不要标成第二声（ˊ）。

【Illustration 2】

In writing, when two syllables are in the third tone, the first syllable remains marked as a third tone rather than being changed to the second tone.

lǎohǔ	hǎidǎo	huǒbǎ
老虎（tiger）	海岛（island）	火把（torch）
jiǔ diǎn	shuǐguǎn	wǔdǎo
九点（nine O'clock）	水管（water pipe）	舞蹈（dancing）
xiǎogǒu	xǐ liǎn	nǐ hǎo
小狗（puppy）	洗脸（wash face）	你好（How are you）

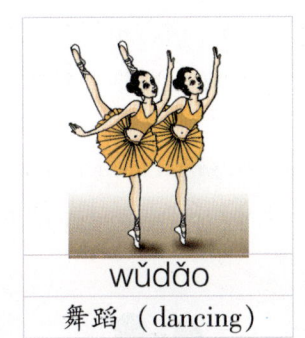

🍄 **三个第三声音节相连时的变调**

（Third-tone Sandhi of Three Syllables in the Third Tone）

🌵 说明

由 A、B、C 三个第三声音节组成词语或组合在一起，该怎么读呢？我们根据其在语法、语义上的关系，可以把它切分为 A/BC 和 AB/C 两种

第六课　第三声的变调

形式。

【Illustration】

How to read three syllables in the third tone when they immediately follow one another? Two formats—A/BC and AB/C—shall be examined according to their relationship in grammar and semantics.

A/BC 是指后两个第三声音节在语法或语义上连接比较紧密。它的变调规律是：A 由第三声变成一个低降调，B 由第三声变成第二声，C 仍旧保持第三声，不发生变化。

Format A/BC indicates that the last syllables "BC" are tight in grammar and semantics. The regularity of the third-tone sandhi is that the first syllable "A" shall be marked with a low falling tone (fourth tone), the second syllable "B" shall be marked with the second tone, and the third syllable "C" shall be marked with the same tone.

mǐlǎoshǔ 米/老鼠 Mickey mouse	xiǎo mǔzhǐ 小/拇指 *pinky*	mǎi shuǐguǒ 买/水果 Buy fruit
zhǔ shuǐjiǎo 煮/水饺 boil dumplings	yǒu lǐxiǎng 有/理想 dream of	shuǐ hěn lěng 水/很冷 The water is very cold

AB/C 是指前两个第三声音节在语法或语义上连接比较紧密。它的变调规律是：A 由第三声变成第二声，B 由第三声变成一个低降调，BC 仍旧保持第三声，不发生变化。

Format AB/C indicates that the first two syllables "AB" are tight in grammar and semantics. The regularity of third-tone sandhi is that the first syllable "A" shall be marked with the second tone, the second syllable "B" shall be marked with a low falling tone (fourth tone), and the third syllable "C" shall be marked with the same tone.

pǎomǎchǎng	zǒngtǒngfǔ	dǎnxiǎoguǐ
跑马/场	总统/府	胆小/鬼
horse-racing course	Presidential palace	coward

zhǎnlǎnguǎn	xǐzǎoshuǐ	wǎng běi zǒu
展览/馆	洗澡/水	往北/走
exhibition hall	bathing water	head northward

第六课　第三声的变调

练习（Exercises）

一、听录音，跟读下面的拼音，注意第三声在非第三声音节前的变调：

Listen and read after the tape; pay attention to the sandhi of the third tone when the third tone is in front of three other third tones.

lǎoshī	hǎochī	huǒchē	mǔqīn
老师	好吃	火车	母亲
teacher	tasty	train	mother

kěnéng	qǐlái	xiǎoshí	yǐqián
可能	起来	小时	以前
possible	get up	hour	before

guǎnggào	bǐsài	fǎnduì	fǎngwèn
广告	比赛	反对	访问
advertisement	match	oppose	visit

二、听录音，跟读下面的拼音，注意第三声在第三声音节前的变调：

Listen and read after the tape; pay attention to the sandhi of the third tone in front of the other tones.

dǎrǎo	guǎngchǎng	kěyǐ	liǎojiě
打扰	广场	可以	了解
disturb	square	may	know

lǎobǎn	lěngyǐn	shǒuzhǐ	yǔsǎn
老板	冷饮	手纸	雨伞
boss	cold drink	toilet paper	umbrella

zhǐhǎo	zǎodiǎn	yǒngyuǎn	yǒuhǎo
只好	早点	永远	友好
have to	breakfast	forever	friendly

三、听录音，跟读下面的拼音，注意三个第三声音节连读的变调：

Listen and read after the tape; pay attention to the third-tone sandhi of three syllables in the third tone.

mǎi bǎoxiǎn	zhǎo fǔdǎo	jiǎng yǔfǎ	wǒ xiǎng nǐ
买/保险	找/辅导	讲/语法	我/想你
buy insurance	want a tutor	explain grammar	I miss you

chǔlǐpǐn	guǎnlǐzhě	lǎobǎnyǐ	gǎnjǐn zǒu
处理/品	管理/者	老板/椅	赶紧/走
goods sold at reduced prices	manager	boss chair	in a hurry

四、试着朗读下面全部由第三声音节组成的句子：

Try to read aloud the following sentence consisting of syllables in the third tone.

Nǐ xiǎng mǎi nǎ zhǒng bǎoxiǎn?
你 想 买 哪 种 保险？What insurance do you want to have?

Wǎng běi zǒu jǐ bǎi mǐ yǒu lǚguǎn.
往 北 走 几 百 米 有 旅馆。
A restaurant is several hundred meters to the north of here.

五、朗读下面的绕口令,注意第三声的变调:

Read aloud the following tongue twisters and pay attention to the third-tone sandhi.

Gǔ shàng huà lǎohǔ,
鼓 上 画 老虎,Draw a tiger on a drum
nòngpò ná bù bǔ.
弄 破 拿 布 补。Mend it with a piece of cloth when it is torn
Bù zhī shì bù bǔ gǔ,
不 知 是 布补鼓,Whether mend the drum with the piece of cloth
háishì bù bǔ hǔ.
还是 布 补 虎。Or mend the tiger with the piece of cloth

第七课 汉语拼音的音节结构与拼写规则

Lesson Seven Syllable Structure and Spelling Rules of *Pinyin*

汉语拼音的音节结构（Syllable Structure of *Pinyin*）

说明 1

汉语拼音的音节可分为声母和韵母两大部分，声调贯穿于整个音节。其中，韵母又可分为韵头、韵腹和韵尾三部分。其中，韵腹是必不可少的。如下表：

【Illustration 1】

Most syllables in Chinese are composed of initials and finals; all syllables have a tone. Finals can be divided into three parts: head final, essential final and tail final. Among the three parts, the essential final is indispensable. See the following form.

音节	声母 initials （辅音声母21个）	声调（ˉ、ˊ、ˇ、ˋ） tone			
		韵母 finals			
		韵头 head vowel i、u、ü	韵腹 essential vowel a、o、e、i、u、ü	韵尾 tail vowel i、u、-n、-ng	

组成\举例	声母 initials	韵母 finals			声调 tone
		韵头 head vowel	韵腹 essential vowel	韵尾 tail vowel	
我 I		u	o		第三声 the third tone
爱 love			a	i	第四声 the fourth tone
你 you	n		i		第三声 the third tone

说明 2

汉语拼音中并非任何声母都可以和任何韵母相拼，并非声韵母相拼后都有四个声调。如，声母 j、q、x 不能和 a、o、e、u 开头的韵母相拼，但是能和 i、ü 开头的韵母相拼。又如，deng 这一音节在实际发音中有第一声、第三声和第四声，但是没有第二声。

【Illustration 2】

Not every initial can be matched to a final in *pinyin*. Not every syllable has each of the four tones. For example, "j", "q" or "x" cannot match finals beginning with "a", "o", "e" or "u", but they can match those beginning with "i" or "ü". Another example, the syllable "deng" has only the first, third and fourth tones, not the second tone.

dēng
灯（light）

✗

děng
等（wait）

dèng
瞪（stare）

汉语拼音的拼写规则 (Spelling Rules of *Pinyin*)

关于字母 y 和 w 的用法小结 (Summary of the usage of "y" and "w")

说明 1

i 和 i 开头的韵母自成音节时，除了 i、in、ing 三个音节要在 i 前面加 y 以外，其他一律把 i 改写为 y。如：yi, yin, ying; ya, ye, you, yong。

【Illustration 1】

When the final "i" and a final beginning with "i" acts as a syllable, the final "i" changes to "y" and the three syllables "i", "in" and "ing" shall have "y" placed before them. Examples: "yi", "yin", "ying"; "ya", "ye", "you", "yong".

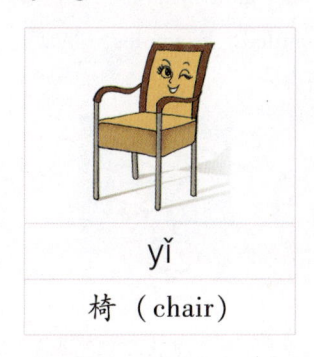

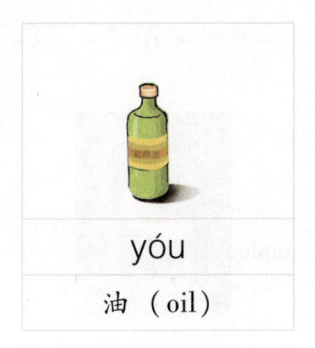

yǐ	yóu	yīng
椅（chair）	油（oil）	鹰（eagle）

说明 2

u 和 u 开头的韵母自成音节时，除了在韵母 u 前面要加 w 以外，其他一律把 u 改写为 w。如：wu, wa, wei, wen, weng。

【Illustration 2】

When the final "u" acts as a syllable, "w" shall be added before the final "u". When finals begin with "u" act as syllables, the final "u" changes to "w". Example: "wu", "wa", "wei", "wen", "weng".

wǔ	wèn	wǎng
五（five）	问（ask）	网（net）

🌵 说明 3

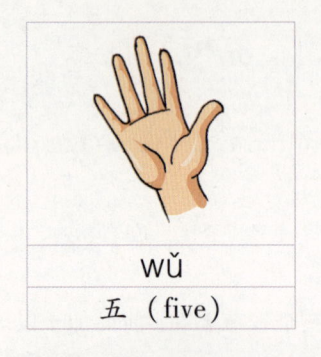

ü 和 ü 开头的韵母自成音节时，一律在 ü 的前面加上 y，并省略 ü 上的两点。如：yu, yue, yun。

【Illustration 3】

When the final "ü" and finals beginning with "ü" act as a syllable, "y" is placed before "ü" and the two dots above "ü" are omitted. Examples："yu", "yue" and "yun".

yú	yuè	yún
鱼（fish）	月（moon）	云（cloud）

关于 iou、uei、uen 的略写小结（Summary on simplifying "iou", "uei" and "uen"）

🌵 说明

当 iou、uei、uen 这三个韵母前面拼上声母组成音节时，其中的 o、e 省略不写。需要注意的是，只是省略不写，但是在发音时，还要把 o、e 的音发出来。但当它们自成音节时，只将 i 改写成 y，u 改写成 w，中间的 o、e 不能省略。如：ji(o)u, shu(e)i, gu(e)n; you, wei, wen。

72

【 Illustration 】

When a syllable consists of an initial and one of the three finals "iou", "uei" or "uen", "o" or "e" is omitted when writing the pinyin. However, we should include them in the pronunciation when we speak. When "iou", "uei" or "uen" act as a syllable, "i" becomes "y" and "u" becomes "w" without omitting "o" or "e" in the center place. Examples: "ji (o) u", "shu (e) i", "gu (e) n", "you", "wei" and "wen".

jiǔ	shuì	gǔn
酒 (alcoholic drink)	睡 (sleep)	滚 (roll)
yóu	wèi	wěn
游 (swim)	喂 (feed)	吻 (kiss)

汉语拼音的标调法小结 (Summary of marking tones in *pinyin*)

汉语拼音的声调一般标在 a、o、e、i、u、ü 等元音字母的上面，如果在一个音节中出现上述两个以上的元音字母，标调时要按以下顺序：（1）a；（2）o 或 e；（3）i、u、ü。标调时要按这一顺序，也就是说，如果韵母中有 a，无论其位置在前在后，都要将声调标在 a 的上面。在没有 a 的情况下，再考虑 e 或 o（二者不会同时出现），最后考虑 i、u、ü。iou 和 uei 前边有声母时，中间的 o 和 e 被省略了，因此，本应该标在 o 和 e 上的声调顺延，标在后面的 u 和 i 上。

　　Usually the tone is marked above the initials "a", "o", "e", "i", "u" or "ü". In case of two initials appearing in the same syllable, the tone shall be marked in the following order: (1) a; (2) o or e; (3) i, u, ü. That is to say, the tone mark shall be always above "a" no matter where it appears in the syllable. When a syllable consists of an initial and one of the three finals "iou", "uei", and "ien", "o" or "e" will be omitted in writing, and the tone mark shall placed above "u" or "i".

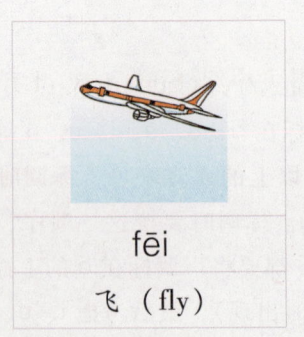

tǎ	tù	nǔ
塔（tower）	兔（rabbit）	女（female）

biǎo	hǎi	huā
表（watch）	海（sea）	花（flower）

hóu	fēi	biě
猴（monkey）	飞（fly）	瘪（flat）

guī	niú
龟 (turtle)	牛 (cattle)

隔音符号（Syllable-diving mark）

说明

以 a、o、e 开头的音节连接在其他音节后面时，如果音节之间的界限发生了混淆，需要使用隔音符号（'）把它们分开。在使用电脑键盘打字时，应特别注意这一点。如：

【Illustration】

When syllables beginning with "a", "o" or "e" follow other syllables, the syllable-dividing mark (') shall be used if there is confusion.

xiān	Xī'ān	jiě	jī'è
先	西安	姐	饥饿
first	Xī'ān	elder sister	hungry

piào	pí'ǎo	kuài	kù'ài
票	皮袄	快	酷爱
ticket	leather coat	quick	love ardently

míngē	míng'é	dāngàn	dàng'àn
民歌	名额	单干	档案
folk song	the number of people allowed	do sth. single-handed	files

fǎngǎn	fāng'àn
反感	方案
dislike	scheme

第七课　音节结构与拼写规则

附录1 普通话声韵配合音节表

声\韵	以 a，o，e 开头的韵母												
	a	o	e	ai	ei	ao	ou	an	en	ang	eng	ong	-i
b	ba	bo		bai	bei	bao		ban	ben	bang	beng		
p	pa	po		pai	pei	pao	pou	pan	pen	pang	peng		
m	ma	mo	me	mai	mei	mao	mou	man	men	mang	meng		
f	fa	fo			fei		fou	fan	fen	fang	feng		
d	da		de	dai	dei	dao	dou	dan	den	dang	deng	dong	
t	ta		te	tai	tei	tao	tou	tan		tang	teng	tong	
n	na		ne	nai	nei	nao	nou	nan	nen	nang	neng	nong	
l	la		le	lai	lei	lao	lou	lan		lang	leng	long	
g	ga		ge	gai	gei	gao	gou	gan	gen	gang	geng	gong	
k	ka		ke	kai	kei	kao	kou	kan	ken	kang	keng	kong	
h	ha		he	hai	hei	hao	hou	han	hen	hang	heng	hong	
j													
q													
x													
z	za		ze	zai	zei	zao	zou	zan	zen	zang	zeng	zong	zi
c	ca		ce	cai	cei	cao	cou	can	cen	cang	ceng	cong	ci
s	sa		se	sai		sao	sou	san	sen	sang	seng	song	si
zh	zha		zhe	zhai	zhei	zhao	zhou	zhan	zhen	zhang	zheng	zhong	zhi
ch	cha		che	chai		chao	chou	chan	chen	chang	cheng	chong	chi
sh	sha		she	shai	shei	shao	shou	shan	shen	shang	sheng		shi
r			re			rao	rou	ran	ren	rang	reng	rong	ri

附录2　普通话声韵配合音节表

韵\声	以 i 开头的韵母									以 ü 开头的韵母			
	i	ia	ie	iao	iou(iu)	ian	in	iang	ing	iong	ü	üe	üan	ün
b	bi		bie	biao		bian	bin		bing					
p	pi		pie	piao		pian	pin		ping					
m	mi		mie	miao	miu	mian	min		ming					
f														
d	di	dia	die	diao	diu	dian			ding					
t	ti		tie	tiao		tian			ting					
n	ni		nie	niao	niu	nian	nin	niang	ning		nü	nüe		
l	li	lia	lie	liao	liu	lian	lin	liang	ling		lü	lüe		
g														
k														
h														
j	ji	jia	jie	jiao	jiu	jian	jin	jiang	jing	jiong	ju	jue	juan	jun
q	qi	qia	qie	qiao	qiu	qian	qin	qiang	qing	qiong	qu	que	quan	qun
x	xi	xia	xie	xiao	xiu	xian	xin	xiang	xing	xiong	xu	xue	xuan	xun
z														
c														
s														
zh														
ch														
sh														
r														

附录3 普通话声韵配合音节表

声\韵	以 u 开头的韵母								
	u	ua	uo	uai	uei (ui)	uan	uen(un)	uang	ueng
b	bu								
p	pu								
m	mu								
f	fu								
d	du		duo		dui	duan	dun		
t	tu		tuo		tui	tuan	tun		
n	nu		nuo			nuan	nun		
l	lu		luo			luan	lun		
g	gu	gua	guo	guai	gui	guan	gun	guang	
k	ku	kua	kuo	kuai	kui	kuan	kun	kuang	
h	hu	hua	huo	huai	hui	huan	hun	huang	
j									
q									
x									
z	zu		zuo		zui	zuan	zun		
c	cu		cuo		cui	cuan	cun		
s	su		suo		sui	suan	sun		
zh	zhu	zhua	zhuo	zhuai	zhui	zhuan	zhun	zhuang	
ch	chu	chua	chuo	chuai	chui	chuan	chun	chuang	
sh	shu	shua	shuo	shuai	shui	shuan	shun	shuang	
r	ru	rua	ruo		rui	ruan	run		

练习（Exercises）

一、听录音，跟读下面的声母和韵母：

Listen to the tape and read the following *pinyin* after the tape.

b	p	m	f
g	k	h	
zh	ch	sh	r

d	t	n	l
j	q	x	
z	c	s	

a	ai	an	ang	ao				
o	ong	ou						
e	ei	en	eng					
i	ia	ian	iang	iao	ie	in	ing	iong	iou
u	ua	uai	uan	uang	uei	uen	ueng	uo
ü	üe	üan	ün					

二、听写拼音（包括声调），注意 y、w 的使用：

Listen and write down the *pinyin* (including tones) you hear. Pay attention to the usage of "y" and "w".

1.	2.	3.	4.	5.	6.	7.	8.
9.	10.	11.	12.	13.	14.	15.	16.

三、听录音，在与听到的拼音一致的答案后面画√：

Listen to the tape and write "√" after the *pinyin* you hear.

第七课　音节结构与拼写规则

1.	gè	kè	guò	kuò
2.	gǒng	jiǒng	zhǒng	zǒng
3.	rì	lì	shì	rè
4.	huā	fā	hā	huō
5.	tè	duò	tuò	ruò
6.	cáng	chán	cán	cháng
7.	bīn	bēng	bīng	bēn
8.	gōng	gēng	kōng	kēng
9.	cì	cù	sì	sù
10.	jiāo	zhāo	qiāo	chāo
11.	qù	jù	qì	jì
12.	zì	jì	rì	zhì

四、听录音，将下面拼音中缺少的声母补上：

Listen to the tape and fill in the blanks with the missing initials.

1. ___ài	2. ___éi	3. ___ān	4. ___òu	5. ___áng
6. ___ǎo	7. ___üē	8. ___ūn	9. ___uàn	10. ___iǎ
11. ___uò	12. ___uāi	13. ___iǔ	14. ___uì	15. ___uā

五、听录音，将下列拼音中缺少的复韵母补上并加上声调：

Listen to the tape and fill in the blanks with the missing compound finals and tones.

1. z___	2. sh___	3. n___	4. t___	5. p___
6. g___	7. f___	8. zh___	9. q___	10. j___
11. h___	12. l___	13. x___	14. ch___	15. d___

六、将下面表格中的声母、韵母和声调拼合在一起，组成完整的拼音：

Write down the complete *pinyin* using the given initials, finals and tones.

1.	q	iou	-		6.	x	üan	-
2.	j	iao	´		7.	h	uei	`
3.	sh	ou	`		8.	l	ie	ˇ
4.	x	ün	´		9.	n	üe	`
5.	k	uen	`		10.	m	ei	´

七、朗读下面的拼音，注意音节中的隔音符号：

Read aloud the following pinyin and pay attention to the syllable-dividing marks in the syllables.

bēi'āi	hé'ǎi	liàn'ài	xǐ'ài
悲哀	和蔼	恋爱	喜爱
sad	kindly	be in love	like

píng'ān	hēi'àn	mián'ǎo	jiāo'ào
平安	黑暗	棉袄	骄傲
safe and sound	dark	cotton-padded jacket	proud

jīn'é	zuì'è	xī'ōu	pèi'ǒu
金额	罪恶	西欧	配偶
sum of money	evil	Western Europe	spouse

八、读下面的句子，注意声调的区别：

Read the following sentences and pay attention to the differences of tones.

Wǒ yào shuǐjiǎo。

我 要 水饺。I want dumplings

Wǒ yào shuì jiào。

我 要 睡觉。I want to sleep

九、朗读下面的谜语，猜猜说的是什么.

Read aloud the following riddle and try to solve the riddle.

Yuǎn kàn shān yǒu sè,

远 看 山 有 色, Seen from far away, the mountain has colors

jìn tīng shuǐ wú shēng.

近听 水 无 声。Heard from the near place, the water is silent

Chūn qù huā hái zài,

春 去花 还 在,

The flower is still coming into bloom though spring is over

rén lái niǎo bù jīng.

人 来 鸟 不 惊。Birds are not surprised at people's arrival

第八课 "一"和"不"的变调

Lesson Eight Tone Sandhi of "一" and "不"

"一" 的变调 (Tone Sandhi of "一")

说明 1

"一"作为独立音节时读原调 yī。

【Illustration 1】

"一" shall be read in its original tone "yī" as an individual syllable.

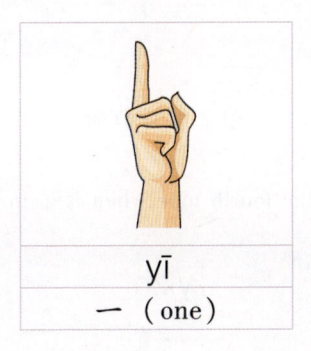

yī
一 （one）

说明 2

"一"用在词的末尾时也读原调 yī。

【Illustration 2】

"一" shall also be read in its original tone "yī" when it comes at the end of a word.

wànyī	wéiyī	tǒngyī
万一	唯一	统一
in case	only	unite

🌵 说明 3

"一"在第四声音节前，变为第二声 yí。

【Illustration 3】

When in a word, "一" shall be read in the second tone "yí" when it is in front of a syllable with the fourth tone.

yíyàng	yíqiè	yídìng
一样	一切	一定
same	everything	must
yígòng	yíwàn	yí wèi
一共	一万	一位
altogether	ten thousand	one person

🌵 说明 4

"一"在第一声、第二声和第三声音节前，变为四声 yì。

【Illustration 4】

"一" shall be read in the fourth tone when it is in front of the first, second or third tone.

yìbān	yìzhí	yìqǐ
一般	一直	一起
common	always	together
yì bēi	yì píng	yìbǎi
一杯	一瓶	一百
a cup of	a bottle of	hundred

说明 5

"一"作序数词时，表示"第一"的排序，即使处在第一声、第二声和第三声音节前，也不能变调，仍读作原调 yī。

【Illustration 5】

"一" shall be read in its original tone "yī" when it acts as an ordinal number to show "Number One".

yī bān	yī niánjí	Běijīng Yī Zhōng
一班	一年级	北京一中
Class One	Grade One	The first middle school of Beijing

yī hào	yī céng	dìyī míng
一号	一层	第一名
the first day of the month	the first floor	the first place

说明 6

在汉语词典中，为简便起见，条目中的"一"一般习惯上都标为 yī。在汉语教材中，一般根据实际发音标调。

【Illustration 6】

To simplify, "一" is marked in the first tone "yī" in all entries in the Chinese Dictionary. While in Chinese Textbooks, it is marked depending on the pronunciation.

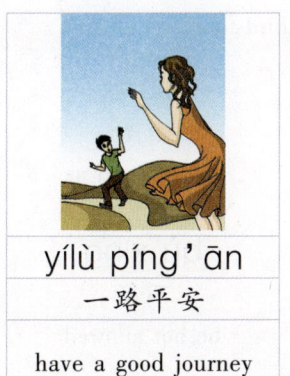

yíjiànzhōngqíng	yílù píng'ān	wànzhòng yìxīn
一见钟情	一路平安	万众一心
fall in love at the first sight	have a good journey	all of one heart

"不"的变调 (Tone Sandhi of "不")

说明 1

"不"单独念或用在词句末尾都读原调 bù。

【Illustration 1】

"不" shall also be read in its original tone "bù" when it occurs by itself or it as at the end of a word.

bù
不 (no)

说明 2

"不"在第一声、第二声和第三声音节前，仍读第四声 bù。

【Illustration 2】

In disyllables, "不" shall also be read in the fourth tone "bù" when it is in front of the first, second or third tone.

bù'ān	bùrú	bùjiǔ
不安	不如	不久
disturbed	not as good as	soon

bù hē	bù xíng	bù hǎo
不喝	不行	不好
not drink	be not allowed	bad

说明 3

"不"在第四声音节前,变为第二声 bú。

【Illustration 3】

"不" shall be read in the second tone in disyllables as well as when it is followed by other words in the fourth tone.

búdàn	búcuò	búyào
不但	不错	不要
not only	good	not want

búyòng	bú qù	bú duì
不用	不去	不对
need not	not go	wrong

说明 4

在汉语词典中,为简便起见,条目中的"不"一般习惯上都标为 bù。在汉语教材中,一般根据实际发音标调。

【Illustration 4】

To simplify, "不" is marked in the second tone "bù" in all entries in Chinese Dictionary. While in Chinese Textbooks, it is marked depending on the factual pronunciation.

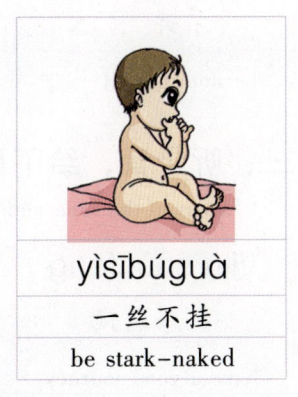

bùxiāngshàngxià	mènmènbúlè	yìsībúguà
不相上下	闷闷不乐	一丝不挂
equally matched	depressed	be stark-naked

练习（Exercises）

一、听录音，跟读下面的拼音，注意"一"的变调：

Listen and read the following *pinyin* after the tape; pay attention to the tone sandhi of "一".

yíbàn	yídào	yìbiān	yìqí
一半	一道	一边	一齐
half	together	one side	altogether

yìshēng	yìtóng	yízài	yìkǒuqì
一生	一同	一再	一口气
all one's life	together	again and again	without a break

二、听录音，跟读下面的拼音，注意"不"的变调：

Listen and read the following *pinyin* after the tape; pay attention to tone sandhi of "不".

búduàn	bùguǎn	búlùn	bùgǎndān
不断	不管	不论	不敢当
continuous	despite	however	I really don't deserve this.

bùxǔ	búshì	búguò	bú yàojǐn
不许	不是	不过	不要紧
be not allowed	be not	but	It doesn't matter

三、听录音，给下面音节中的"yi"加上声调：

Listen to the tape and add tones to "yi" in the following *pinyin*.

yilù shùnfēng	yijǔ liǎngdé	yirì sānqiū
一路顺风	一举两得	一日三秋
have a good journey	gain two ends at once	Days creep by like years

yishìtóngrén	yīfānfēngshùn	yìxīn yíyì
一视同仁	一帆风顺	一心一意
treat equally without discrimination	Everything is going smoothly	concentrated heart and soul

四、听录音，给下面音节中的"bu"加上声调：

Listen to the tape and add tones to "bu" in the following *pinyin*.

bucíerbié	buxiāngshàngxià	shuōyī buèr
不辞而别	不相上下	说一不二
leave without saying good-bye	equally matched	stand by one's words

qíngbuzìjīn	buzhī bujué	bubēi bukàng
情不自禁	不知不觉	不卑不亢
cannot help oneself	unconsciously	neither haughty nor humble

五、按照"一"的变调规则，给下面音节中的"yi"加上声调：

Add tones to "yi" in the following pinyin according to the rules of the tone sandhi of "一".

yizhāo yixī	yimúyiyàng	yidiǎn yidī
一朝一夕	一模一样	一点一滴
in one morning or evening	be exactly alike	bit by bit

yiwèn yidá	yishēng yishì	yisī yiháo
一问一答	一生一世	一丝一毫
answer each question successively	in all one's life	a tiny bit

六、按照"不"的变调规则，给下面音节中的"bu"加上声调：
Add tones to "bu" in the following pinyin according to the rules of the tone sandhi of "不".

bùduō bùshǎo	bùféi bùshòu	bùzhé bùkòu
不多不少	不肥不瘦	不折不扣
neither too much nor too little	neither fat nor thin	Hundred-percent/to the letter

bújiàn búsàn	bùyán bùyǔ	bùlěng búrè
不见不散	不言不语	不冷不热
not leave without seeing each other	keep silent	neither hot nor cold

七、请按照实际发音修正下面音节中的"一"和"不"的标音：
Correct the tones of "一" and "不" according to their actual pronunciations.

yìxìliè	yìtiáoxīn	yílǎnbiǎo
一系列	一条心	一览表
a series of	be of one mind	schedule

yìbǎshǒu	yícìxìng	yī shì yī, èr shì èr
一把手	一次性	一是一，二是二
chief	once only	one is one, and two is two/ carefully

bùxiànghuà	bù déyǐ	bú'èrjià
不像话	不得已	不二价
unreasonable	be forced to	uniform price

bùxiùgāng	bùyàoliǎn	bùzàihū
不锈钢	不要脸	不在乎
stainless steel	shameless	not care

八、朗读下面的字谜,注意"不"的读音,并猜猜是什么字:

Read aloud the following riddle about a character; pay attention to the pronunciations of "不" and guess what the character is.

Yí gè bù chū tóu,
一个不出头,One "不" with a stroke over its top

liǎng gè bù chū tóu.
两个不出头,Two "不" each with a stroke over its top

Bú shì bù chū tóu,
不是不出头,Neither of the two "不" hasn't a stroke over its top

jiù shì bù chū tóu.
就是不出头。Only the "不" with a stroke over its top

第八课 "一"和"不"的变调

第九课　卷舌韵母与儿化韵

Lesson Nine　Retroflex Finals and Suffixation of the Nonsyllabic "r"

卷舌韵母（Retroflex Finals）

说明 1

汉语拼音的卷舌韵母有 1 个。

【Illustration 1】

There is only one retroflex final in *pinyin*.

er

说明 2

发这个音时，先发 e，然后把舌头由低到高，由前向后卷起。但是 èr（二）的发音读如"àr"。

【Illustration 2】

When pronouncing "er", first pronounce "e", then raise and retract the tongue backwards. The pronunciation of "èr（二）" will sound like "àr".

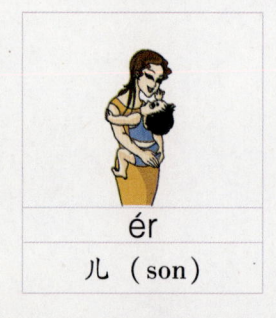

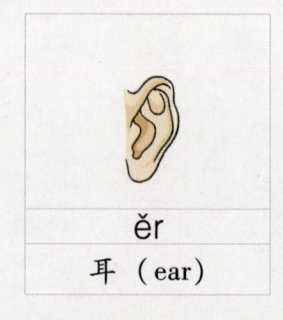

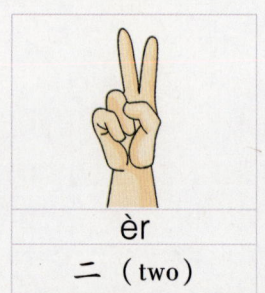

ér	ěr	èr
儿（son）	耳（ear）	二（two）

nǔ'ér
女儿（daughter）

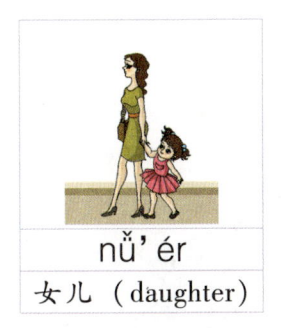

ěrjī
耳机（earphone）

yòu'éryuán
幼儿园(kindergarten)

儿化韵（Suffixation of the Nonsyllabic "r"）

什么是儿化韵（Definition of Suffixation of the nonsyllabic "r"）

卷舌韵母 er 附在别的音节后边，使这个音节的韵母发生变化，成为一个带卷舌动作的韵母，这就是"儿化韵"。写汉语拼音时，在原音节后加上 r。如：huār，就是在发 ua 的时候，a 加上一个卷舌的动作。

When the retroflex vowel "er" follows another syllable, the final of the syllable becomes a retroflex final. This is referred to as the suffixation of the nonsyllabic "r". In *pinyin*, "r" shall be placed after the primary syllable. Example："huār" is pronounced by pronouncing "huā" with an act of retracting the tongue towards the back of the mouth.

huār
花儿（flower）

dōur
兜儿（pocket）

儿化韵的变化规律（Transformation Rules of the Suffixation of the nonsyllabic "r"）

说明 1

原韵母的尾音是 a, o, e, u，变成儿化韵时，发尾音时加上一个卷舌的动作。

【Illustration 1】

Syllables having compound finals ending with "a", "o", "e" or "u" and changed with the suffixation of the nonsyllabic "r", are pronounced by retracting the tongue towards the back of the mouth.

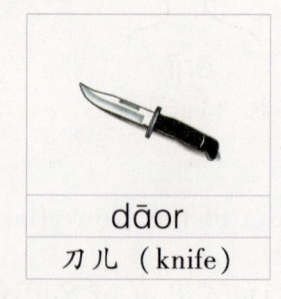

huàr	dāor	hóur
画儿（drawing）	刀儿（knife）	猴儿（monkey）

说明 2

原韵母是 i、ü 和在 z、c、s、zh、ch、sh、r 后的 i，变成儿化韵时，在韵母后加上 e 的音，然后再卷舌。

【Illustration 2】

When finals "i", "ü" and the final "i" following "z", "c", "s", "zh", "ch", "sh", "r" change with the suffixation of the nonsyllabic "r", they are pronounced by first adding an additional "e" and then retracting the tongue towards the back of the mouth when ending the pronunciation.

xiǎojīr	cìr	jīnyúr
小鸡儿（chick）	刺儿（thorn）	金鱼儿（goldfish）

说明 3

原韵母的尾音是 i、n（ün、in 除外），变成儿化韵时，先丢掉尾音 i、n，然后再卷舌。

【Illustration 3】

When finals end with "i" or "n" (except "ün" and "in") change with the suffixation of the nonsyllabic "r", they are pronounced by omitting "i" or "n", and then retracting the tongue when ending the pronunciation.

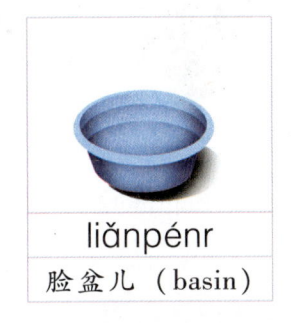

xiāngshuǐr
香水儿（drawing）

liǎnpénr
脸盆儿（basin）

bīnggùnr
冰棍儿(ice cream)

说明 4

原韵母是 ün、in，变成儿化韵时，先丢掉尾音，加上 e 的发音，最后再卷舌。

【Illustration 4】

When finals ending with "ün" and "in" change with the suffixation of the nonsyllabic "r", they are pronounced by omitting the last phonetic symbol, adding "e", and then retracting the tongue towards the back of the mouth when ending the pronunciation.

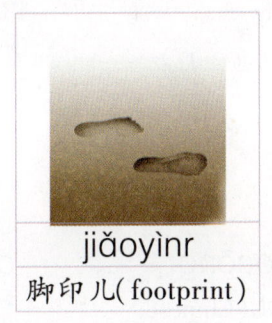

huāqúnr
花裙儿(colored skirt)

jiǎoyìnr
脚印儿(footprint)

说明 5

原韵母是 ing，变成儿化韵时，先丢掉尾音 ng，再加上 e 的发音，最后卷舌。注意：这时，音节中 i 和 e 有鼻化现象。

【Illustration 5】

When the final "ing" changes with the suffixation of the nonsyllabic "r", it is pronounced by omitting the phonetic "ng", adding "e" and then retracting the tongue when ending the pronunciation. Caution: here, "i" and "e" in the syllable shall be nasalized.

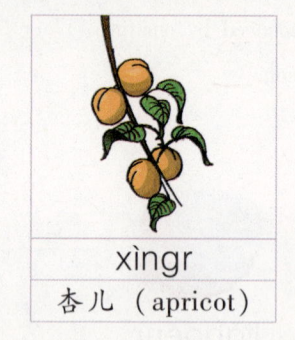

píngr
瓶儿 (bottle)

xìngr
杏儿 (apricot)

diànyǐngr
电影儿 (movie)

说明 6

原韵母的尾音是 ng(ing 除外)，变成儿化韵时，先丢掉尾音 ng，然后卷舌。注意：这时，音节中的韵母有鼻化现象。

【Illustration 6】

When compound finals end with "ng" (except "ing") change with the suffixation of the nonsyllabic "r", they are pronounced by omitting the last phonetic "ng" and retracting the tongue towards the back of the mouth when ending the pronunciation. Caution: There are nasalization phenomena in the syllables.

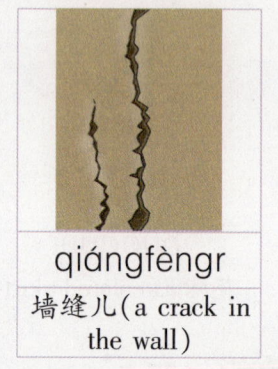

xiǎocōngr
小葱儿 (Chinese green onion)

dànhuángr
蛋黄儿 (yolk)

qiángfèngr
墙缝儿 (a crack in the wall)

儿化韵的作用 (Function of the Suffixation of the nonsyllabic "r")

说明 1

儿化韵可以区别词性,使动词或形容词变成一个名词。如：

【Illustration 1】

The suffixation of the nonsyllabic "r" can help distinguish the parts of speech and turn a verb or adjective into a noun.

huà	huàr	gài	gàir
画 (to paint/draw)	画儿 (painting)	盖 (to cover)	盖儿 (lid/cover)

jiān	jiānr	cuò	cuòr
尖 (sharp)	尖儿 (tip)	错 (wrong)	错儿 (mistakes)

说明 2

儿化韵可以区别词义。如：

【Illustration 2】

The suffixation of the nonsyllabic "r" can help distinguish the meaning of a word.

yì diǎn	yìdiǎnr	yǎn	yǎnr
一点 (one o'clock)	一点儿 (a little)	眼 (eye)	眼儿 (small hole)

sī	sīr	tóu	tóur
丝 (silk)	丝儿 (thread-like thing)	头 (head)	头儿 (leader)

说明 3

儿化韵可以表示小的、可爱的等感情色彩，或表示生活中常见的、不重要的事物。对比一下：

【Illustration 3】

The suffixation of nonsyllabic "r" can express emotive meaning on small and lovely things or on something common and unimportant. Please contrast the following words.

jǐnggùn	bīnggùnr	 shāyú	 jīnyúr
警棍 (baton)	冰棍儿 (ice cream)	鲨鱼 (shark)	金鱼儿 (goldfish)

lánggǒu	xiǎogǒur	hǎishuǐ	xiāngshuǐr
狼狗 (wolf dog)	小狗儿 (puppy)	海水 (sea water)	香水儿 (perfume)

练习（Exercises）

一、听录音，跟读下面的拼音，注意"er"的发音：
Listen and repeat after the tape; pay attention to the pronunciation of "er".

dīnéng'ér	tuō'érsuǒ	hēimù'ěr	értóngjié
低能儿	托儿所	黑木耳	儿童节
mentally disabled child	kindergarten	Jew's ear	the children's day
shǔyī shǔ'èr	shuōyī bú'èr	sānxīn èryì	jiē'èr liánsān
数一数二	说一不二	三心二意	接二连三
be reckoned as one of the best	mean what one says	be of two minds	one after another

二、听录音，跟读下面的拼音，注意韵母尾音在变成儿化韵时的发音变化：

Pay attention to the pronunciation changes with the suffixation of the nonsyllabic "r".

nǎr	yíxiàr	dàhuǒr	miàntiáor
哪儿	一下儿	大伙儿	面条儿
where	in a short while	everybody	noodle

gèr	zhèr	xífùr	xiǎoliǎngkǒur
个儿	这儿	媳妇儿	小两口儿
of a human being (or animal) height	here	wife	young couple

三、听录音，跟读下面的拼音，注意韵母变成儿化韵时的发音变化：

Listen and repeat after the tape; pay attention to the pronunciation changes especially in cases when the finals change with the suffixation of the nonsyllabic "r".

第九课 卷舌韵母与儿化韵

zhēnbír	dùqír	méi shìr	zhír
针鼻儿	肚脐儿	没事儿	侄儿
the eye of a needle	navel	it doesn't matter	nephew
tiāo cìr	guāzǐr	sūnnǚr	xiǎoqǔr
挑刺儿	瓜子儿	孙女儿	小曲儿
find fault with	melon seeds	granddaughter	ditty

四、听录音,跟读下面的拼音,注意韵母尾音在变成儿化韵时的发音变化:

Listen and repeat after the tape; pay attention to the pronunciation changes with the suffixation of the nonsyllabic "r".

mòshuǐr	yíhuìr	xiǎoháir	míngpáir
墨水儿	一会儿	小孩儿	名牌儿
ink	a little while	child	famous brand
liángfěnr	shūběnr	niúròugānr	ménkǎnr
凉粉儿	书本儿	牛肉干儿	门槛儿
bean jelly	books	beef jerky	doorsill

五、听录音,跟读下面的拼音,注意韵母在变成儿化韵时的发音变化:

Listen and repeat after the tape; pay attention to the pronunciation changes especially in cases when the finals change with the suffixation of the nonsyllabic "r".

càidiér	piěr	pèijuér	mùjuér
菜碟儿	撇儿	配角儿	木橛儿
dish	left falling stroke	costar	a short wooden stake

duǎnqúnr	bù héqúnr	dàijìnr	bào xìnr
短裙儿	不合群儿	带劲儿	报信儿
short skirt	unsociable	energetic	inform

六、听录音,跟读下面的拼音,注意韵母在变成儿化韵时的发音变化:

Listen and repeat after the tape; pay attention to the pronunciation changes especially in cases when the finals change into ones with the suffixation of a nonsyllabic "r".

méiyǐngr	yǎnjìngr	shìbǐngr	luósīdīngr
没影儿	眼镜儿	柿饼儿	螺丝钉儿
without a trace	glasses	dried persimmon	screw

七、听录音,跟读下面的拼音,注意韵母尾音在变成儿化韵时的发音变化:

Listen and repeat after the tape; pay attention to the pronunciation changes with the suffixation of the nonsyllabic "r".

shuǐkēngr	xìsǎngr	xiǎoxióngr	hútòngr
水坑儿	细嗓儿	小熊儿	胡同儿
puddle	soft voice	bear	*hutong*

八、听录音,跟读下面的拼音,注意儿化与非儿化词语在词性上的不同:

Listen and repeat after the tape; pay attention to the differences in the parts of speech between the words with or without the suffixation of a nonsyllabic "r".

huó	huór	huǒ	huǒr
活	活儿	火	火儿
alive	job	fire	to be angry

bāo	bāor	cì	cìr
包	包儿	刺	刺儿
wrap	bag	stab	thorn

九、听录音,跟读下面的拼音,注意儿化与非儿化词语在意义上的不同:

Listen and repeat after the tape; pay attention to the differences in meanings between the words with and without the suffixation of the nonsyllabic "r".

xìn	xìnr	nà	nàr
信	信儿	那	那儿
letter	message	that	there

zǎodiǎn	zǎodiǎnr	méijìn	méijìnr
早点	早点儿	没劲	没劲儿
breakfast	earlier	boring	weak

十、听录音,注意儿化音节与非儿化音节意义上的不同:

Listen to the tape and pay attention to the differences in meanings between the words with and without the suffixation of nonsyllabic "r".

guógē	míngēr	bówùguǎn	cháguǎnr
国歌	民歌儿	博物馆	茶馆儿
national anthem	folk song	museum	teahouse

zīběn	jìshìběnr	fāngzhēn	dàtóuzhēnr
资本	记事本儿	方针	大头针儿
capital	notebook	policy	pin

十一、听录音,给下面的词语注音:

Listen to the tape and write down the *pinyin* for the following words.

女儿	馅儿饼	婴儿	水饺儿
daughter	pie	baby	dumpling

聊天儿	好玩儿	儿女	玩意儿
chat	interesting	sons and daughters	plaything

第十课 轻声

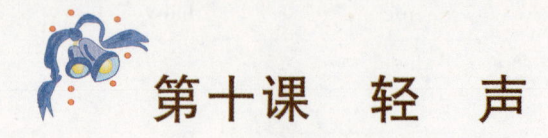

Lesson Ten　Neutral Tone

什么是轻声（What is the Neutral Tone）

说明

　　汉语每个音节都有一定的声调,但是在词或句中,一些音节常会失去原有的声调,而读成一个又轻又短的调子,这种特别的声调就是轻声。

【Illustration】

　　All syllables of Chinese have their own intonations. In some words or sentences, these syllables lose their original intonations and become a light and short intonation. This we call the neutral tone.

轻声的发音（Pronunciation of the Neutral Tone）

　　轻声的实际发音受前一个音节声调高低的影响。

　　The actual pronunciation of the neutral tone is affected by the pitch (or intonation) of the previous syllables.

说明 1

　　前一个音节是第一声,是一个高平调,后边的轻声就比前一个音节低,读作半低调。如下图:

【Illustration 1】

When the first syllable in a word is the first tone (high and flat pitch), and the following syllable of the word is the neutral tone, the following syllable's pitch shall be lower than the previous syllable's pitch (one-half low pitch). See the following pictures.

第一音节 (the first syllable)　　　　第二音节 (the second syllable)

bēizi
杯子 (cup)

xīngxing
猩猩 (orangutan)

xiānsheng
先生 (sir)

说明 2

前一个音节是第二声，是一个上升的高调，后边的轻声就比前一个音节稍微低一些，读作中调。如下图：

【Illustration 2】

When the first syllable in a word is the second tone (rising high pitch), and the following syllable of the word is in the neutral tone, the pitch of the second tone shall be a bit lower than the previous tone (medium pitch). See the following pictures.

第一音节 (the first syllable)　　　　第二音节 (the second syllable)

shítou	bízi	méimao
石头（stone）	鼻子（nose）	眉毛（brow）

说明 3

前一个音节是第三声，是一个先降后升的声调，后边的轻声就顺着前一个音节高上去，读作半高调。如下图：

【Illustration 3】

When the first syllable in a word is the third tone (first falling and then rising pitch) and the following syllable of the word is in the neutral tone, the following syllable shall become higher in pitch than the previous syllable (half high pitch). See the following pictures.

第一音节（the first syllable）　　　　第二音节（the second syllable）

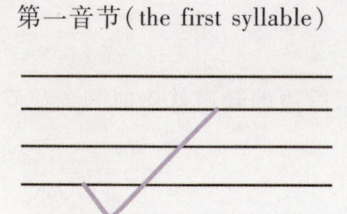

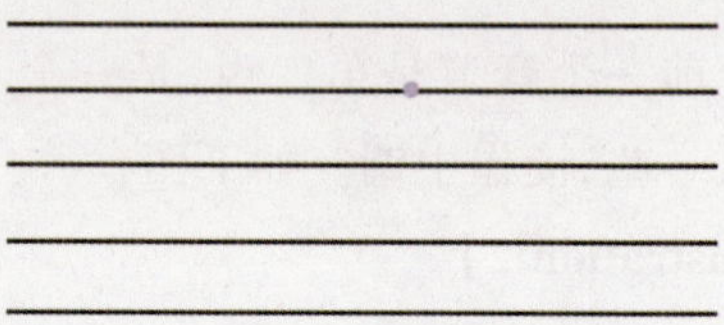

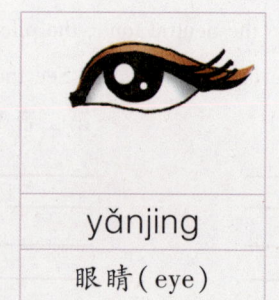

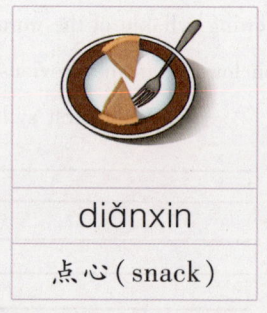

wěiba	yǎnjing	diǎnxin
尾巴（tail）	眼睛（eye）	点心（snack）

另外，两个第三声音节组成的词语，当第二个音节读作轻声时，第一个音节由原来的第三声变为一个低降调。如下图：

Moreover, when some words consist of two syllables in the third tone, the second syllable is read in the neutral tone and the first syllable's pitch in the third tone becomes a low falling pitch. See the following pictures.

第一音节（the first syllable）　　　　第二音节（the second syllable）

jiějie
姐姐（elder sister）

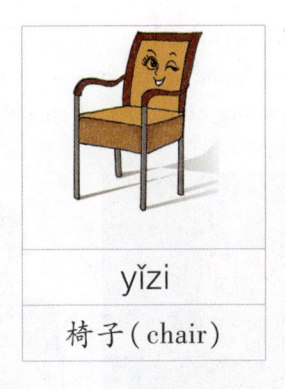

nǎinai
奶奶（grandma）

yǐzi
椅子（chair）

说明 4

前一个音节是第四声，是一个高降调，后边的轻声音节就顺着前一个音节低下来，读作低调。如下图：

【Illustration 4】

When the first syllable in a word is in the fourth tone (high falling pitch) and the following syllable of the word is in the neutral tone, the following syllable's pitch shall become a bit lower than its original pitch. See the following pictures.

第一音节（the first syllable）　　　　第二音节（the second syllable）

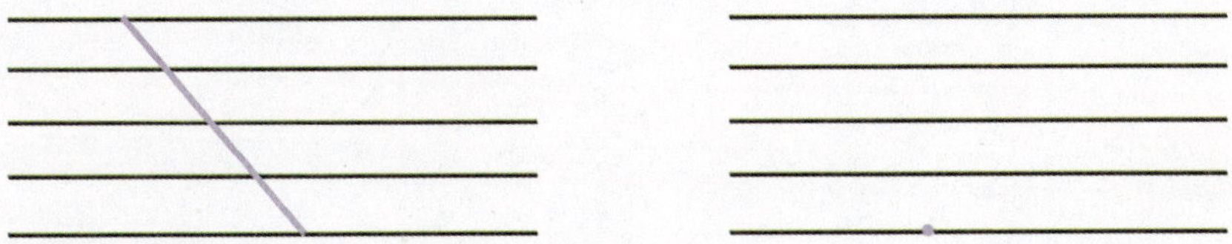

guàntou	kùzi	yuèliang
罐头（can）	裤子（pants）	月亮（moon）

说明

一些词语有两种读音：轻声读法与非轻声读法。这些词语发音不同，所代表的意义和词性往往也不同。

【Illustration】

Some words have two pronunciations: neutral tone and non-neutral tone. The meaning and parts of speech are often different due to the differences of pronunciation.

dìdào	dìdao	lāshǒu	lāshou
地道 tunnel	地道 (form the place well known for a cerain product)	拉手 (hand in hand)	拉手 (handle)

练习 (Exercises)

一、听录音，跟读下面的拼音，注意轻声音节的发音：

Listen and repeat after the tape; pay attention to the pronunciation of the neutral tone.

dōngxi	xiāoxi	gūniang	qīngchu
东西	消息	姑娘	清楚
thing	information	girl	clear

háizi	piányi	késou	liángkuai
孩子	便宜	咳嗽	凉快
child	cheap	cough	cool

xǐhuan	wǎnshang	nǐmen	nuǎnhuo
喜欢	晚上	你们	暖和
like	evening	you	warm

mǎhu	ěrduo	jiǎozi	shěnshen
马虎	耳朵	饺子	婶婶
careless	ear	dumpling	aunt

màozi	àiren	piàoliang	dàifu
帽子	爱人	漂亮	大夫
cap	husband or wife	beautiful	doctor

二、听录音，跟读下面的拼音，注意亲属称呼的正确读音：

Listen and repeat after the tape; pay attention to the correct pronunciation and names of Chinese relatives (aunt, uncle etc).

bàba	māma	yéye	nǎinai
爸爸	妈妈	爷爷	奶奶
dad	mum	grandpa	grandma

第十课 轻声

bóbo	shūshu	gūgu	jiùjiu
伯伯	叔叔	姑姑	舅舅
uncle (father's elder brother)	uncle (father's younger brother)	aunt (father's sister)	uncle (mother's brother)
gēge	dìdi	jiějie	mèimei
哥哥	弟弟	姐姐	妹妹
elder brother	younger brother	elder sister	younger sister

三、听录音,跟读下面的拼音,对比画线词语的读音:

Listen and repeat after the tape; compare the pronunciations of the underlined words.

xǐhuan	liánhuān	yīfu	xīfú
喜欢	联欢	衣服	西服
like	have a get-together	clothes	western-style clothes
mántou	jìngtóu	shíhou	děnghòu
馒头	镜头	时候	等候
mantou (steamed bread)	lens	moment/the duration of time	wait for
àiren	qíngrén	bùfen	bǐfēn
爱人	情人	部分	比分
husband or wife	lover	part	score
fúqi	nuǎnqì	yìsi	xiāngsī
福气	暖气	意思	相思
good fortune	heating	meaning	yearning between lovers

四、听录音,跟读下面的拼音,注意同一词语的不同读法:

Listen and repeat after the tape; pay attention to the different pronunciations of the words that are spelled the same but have different tone marks.

dìfang	dìfāng	rénjia	rénjiā
地方	地方	人家	人家
place	district	other people	household

jīngshen	jīngshén	dàyi	dàyì
精神	精神	大意	大意
vigor	spirit	careless	main idea

yányu	yányǔ	lìhai	lìhài
言语	言语	利害	利害
speak	spoken language	formidable	advantages and disadvantages

五、听录音,在与听到的拼音一致的答案后面画√:

Listen to the tape and write "√" after the *pinyin* you hear.

1.	běnshi	běnshì	6.	rényi	rényì
2.	fǎnzhèng	fǎnzheng	7.	xiàshui	xiàshuǐ
3.	gàosù	gàosu	8.	xiǎozǐ	xiǎozi
4.	gùshi	gùshì	9.	zhàoying	zhàoyìng
5.	méndào	méndao	10.	xiōngdi	xiōngdì

六、听录音,给下面的拼音加上声调,注意拼音中的轻声:

Listen to the tape and add tones to the following *pinyin*. Pay attention to the neutral tones.

zhangfu	youyi	yinwei	xiexie
xiaohair	tianqi	ziji	wanshang
shoushi	shufu	nü'er	mafan

七、朗读下面的拼音,注意轻声音节的读音:

Read aloud the following *pinyin*; pay attention to the pronunciation of the syllables in the neutral tones.

kùnnan	méiyìsi	míngzi	shénme
困难	没意思	名字	什么
difficult	boring	name	what

péngyou	rènshi	shìqing	tāmen
朋友	认识	事情	他们
friend	know	thing	they

tòngkuai	duìbuqǐ	hǎochu	juéde
痛快	对不起	好处	觉得
delighted	sorry	advantage	to feel

八、朗读下面的儿歌,注意轻声音节的读法:

Read aloud the following Children's Song and pay attention to the syllables in the neutral tones.

Zhǎo wa zhǎo wa zhǎo péngyou,
找 哇 找 哇 找 朋友,Look, look, look for a friend

zhǎodào yí ge hǎo péngyou.
找 到 一个 好 朋友。Find a good friend

Jìng ge lǐ, wòwo shǒu,
敬 个礼,握握 手,Give a salute and shakes hands with each other

nǐ shì wǒ de hǎo péngyou.
你是 我的 好 朋友。You are my good friend

Zàijiàn!
再见!Bye-bye

录音文本与参考答案
Tapescript and Answer Key

第一课

一、听录音，把下面的单韵母按听到的顺序写在空格里：

o	e	i	a	ü	u

二、听录音，给下面的拼音加上声调：

1. ó	2. yī	3. yú	4. è	5. ǎ	6. wū
7. yǔ	8. wǔ	9. ǒ	10. à	11. yǐ	12. é

三、听录音，跟读，注意每组拼音的区别：

1.	yí	yú		2.	á	ǎ		3.	wú	wù
4.	ě	ǒ		5.	wù	yù		6.	yǐ	yǔ

四、听录音，按所听到的拼音的顺序在图的下面写上序号：

（一）1~4

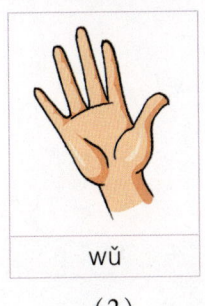

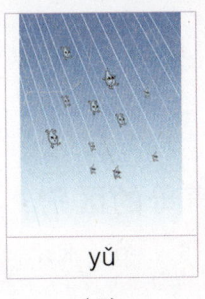

wǔ	yǔ	é	yī
(2)	(4)	(1)	(3)

（二）5～8

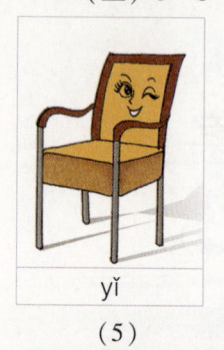

yǐ	è	wū	yú
（5）	（8）	（6）	（7）

七、看图，在图下面的空格里写出相应的拼音：

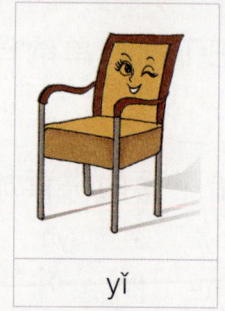

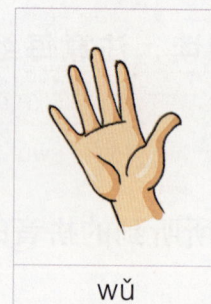

wū	yú	yǐ	yī
é	yǔ	wǔ	è

第二课

一、听录音，跟读，注意每组声母的区别：

1. b p   2. d t   3. g k   4. m n
5. h f   6. b d   7. t f   8. h n

二、听录音，把下面的声母按听到的顺序写在空格里：

b p m f d t n l g k h

1.	g	2.	d	3.	b	4.	l	5.	n	6.	k
7.	p	8.	t	9.	m	10.	f	11.	h		

三、听录音，给下面的拼音加上声调：

bó	gē	nǚ	hé	mā	lǜ	lí	mò
kǎ	lè	pá	nǚ	mò	lǜ	fà	fó

四、听录音，在与听到的拼音一致的答案后面画√：

1.	bó		pó	√	6.	lú		lǔ	√
2.	mǔ	√	mǒ		7.	hā		fā	√
3.	lè		là	√	8.	nǐ		lǐ	√
4.	pā		bā	√	9.	bì	√	dì	
5.	kè	√	gè		10.	nǔ	√	nǔ	

五、听录音，按所听到的词语的顺序在图的下面写上序号：

（一）1~4

pà	mǎ	tǎ	kǎ
（3）	（4）	（2）	（1）

（二）5~8

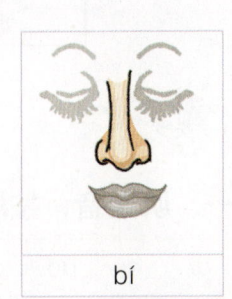

tī	bì	lí	bí
（8）	（7）	（5）	（6）

(三) 9~12

tù	dù	lǜ	nǚ
(11)	(10)	(9)	(12)

八、用连线的方法将下面的图画与相应的拼音连接在一起：

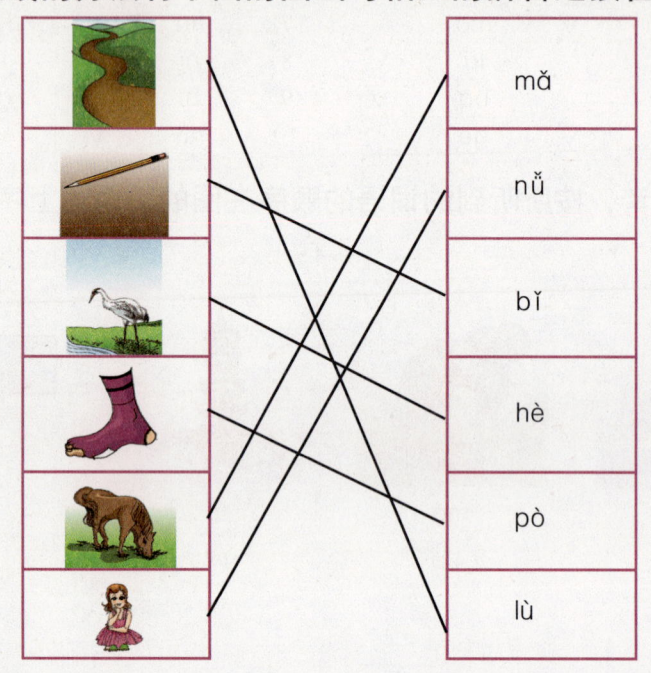

mǎ
nǚ
bǐ
hè
pò
lù

第三课（基础篇）

一、听录音，按所听到的顺序在相应的复韵母的下面写上序号：

ai	ei	ao	ou	ia	ie	iao	iou	ua	uo	uai	uei	üe
6.	9.	10.	8.	1.	3.	7.	4.	13.	12.	2.	5.	11.

116

二、听录音，给下面的拼音加上声调：

1. lái	2. lüè	3. wèi	4. kuài	5. liù	6. guā
7. yè	8. lǎo	9. liǎo	10. yá	11. liè	12. guì
13. yǎo	14. hēi	15. huì	16. wài	17. yóu	18. wǒ

三、听录音，在与听到的拼音一致的答案后面画√：

1. dōu		duō	√	6. nüè	√	niè	
2. niú		liú	√	7. huī		hēi	√
3. diǎ		dǎi	√	8. bǎo		biǎo	√
4. lèi	√	liè		9. biè	√	bèi	
5. kuā	√	kā		10. guài	√	gài	

四、听录音，将下列拼音中缺少的复韵母补上并加上声调：

1. dǎo	2. fǒu	3. kuò	4. nüè	5. liǎ
6. piào	7. miù	8. tiě	9. guǐ	10. bèi

五、比较下面的拼音，在标错声调的拼音右边画×：

1. gǎi		gaǐ	×	6. mào		maò	×
2. huaì	×	huài		7. weì	×	wèi	
3. kuì		kùi	×	8. mìao	×	miào	
4. kūa	×	kuā		9. leì	×	lèi	
5. liù		lìu	×	10. liǎ		lǐa	×

六、将下面的声母与可以搭配的复韵母拼写在一起，填写在下面的表格中：

b + 复韵母

bai	bei	bao	bie	biao

t + 复韵母

tai	tei	tao	tou	tie	tiao	tuo	tui

n + 复韵母

| nai | nei | nao | nou | nie | niao | niu | nuo | nüe |

g + 复韵母

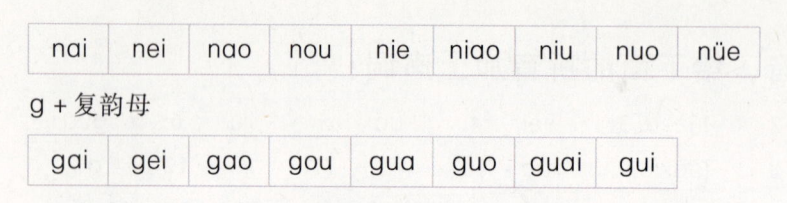

| gai | gei | gao | gou | gua | guo | guai | gui |

九、看图，在图下面的空格里写出相应的拼音：

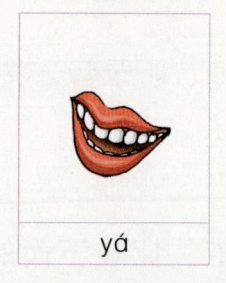

| gǒu | niú | niǎo | māo |

| guī | hóu | ài | yá |

第四课

一、听写声母，将听到的声母按顺序写在下面的空格里：

1.	2.	3.	4.	5.	6.	7.	8.	9.	10.
z	ch	c	j	sh	x	s	q	r	zh

二、听录音，在与听到的拼音一致的答案后面画√：

1.	chā		qiā	√	6.	qué		qié	√
2.	zāi	√	zhāi		7.	ròu		ruò	√
3.	jiǔ		zhǒu	√	8.	rè	√	rù	
4.	jiǎo		qiǎo	√	9.	shǒu		sǒu	√
5.	cuī		suī	√	10.	sì	√	sù	

三、听录音，将下列拼音中缺少的声母补上：

1. _zhuā	2. _cài	3. _jiǔ	4. _shòu	5. _quē
6. _chǎo	7. _xiā	8. _zéi	9. _ruò	10. _suì

四、听两遍录音，根据听到的音节选择下面的声母和韵母，把它们拼写在一起，并加上声调：

cuò	sǎo	zǒu	quē	xié	zhuài	chái	shéi	ruì	jiǎ

五、改正下面拼音中的错误，将正确的拼音写在错误拼音的右边：

1. quē	2. jiǔ	3. yuè	4. yě	5. lüè	6. kuì	7. wǒ	8. yǔ

六、将下面的声母与可以搭配的复韵母拼写在一起，填写在下面的表格中：

sh + 复韵母

shai	shei	shao	shou	shua	shuo	shuai	shui

z + 复韵母

zai	zei	zao	zou	zuo	zui

r + 复韵母

rao	rou	rua	ruo	rui

q + 复韵母

qia	qie	qiao	qiu	que

九、看图，在图下面的空格里写出相应的拼音：

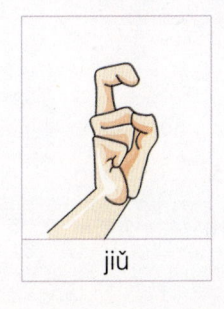

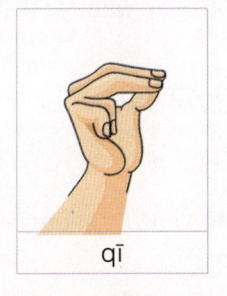

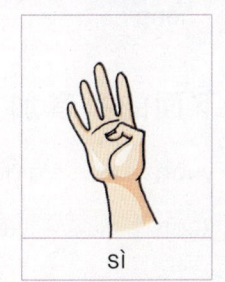

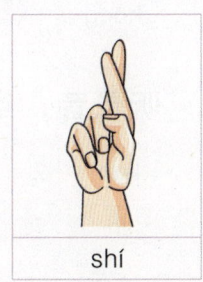

jiǔ	qī	sì	shí

| jī | xiā | zhū | chá |

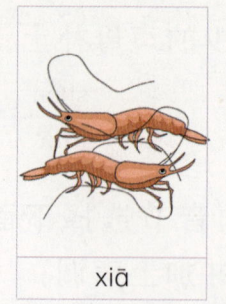

第五课

一、听写韵母，将听到的韵母按顺序写在下面的空格里：

1.	2.	3.	4.	5.	6.	7.	8.
eng	an	ong	uang	ian	iong	uen	iang

9.	10.	11.	12.	13.	14.	15.	16.
uan	ang	ing	en	üan	ueng	in	ün

二、听录音，在与听到的拼音一致的答案后面画√：

1.	chán		cháng	√	6.	lín		líng	√
2.	liǎng	√	liǎn		7.	jǐng		jiǒng	√
3.	wàn	√	wàng		8.	kùn	√	kòng	
4.	yǔn		yǒng	√	9.	yuān	√	yān	
5.	hóng	√	héng		10.	wēn		wēng	√

三、听录音，给下面的拼音加上声调：

1.	lián	2.	yuān	3.	qiǎng	4.	kuáng	5.	xiōng
6.	lìn	7.	kuān	8.	yūn	9.	zhuàn	10.	luàn

四、听两遍录音，给下面由汉字组成的句子加上拼音：

chū	cì	jiàn	miàn		qǐng	duō	guān	zhào	
初	次	见	面	，	请	多	关	照	。

五、将下面表格中的声母和韵母拼合在一起并加上相应的声调，组成完整的拼音：

1.	zh	uo	´	zhuó		6.	j	iou	-	jiū
2.	l	üe	`	lüè		7.	q	üan	´	quán
3.	h	uen	´	hún		8.	z	uei	`	zuì
4.	ch	ou	ˇ	chǒu		9.	f	ei	ˇ	fěi
5.	n	ü	ˇ	nǚ		10.	b	iao	-	biāo

六、用连线的方法将下面的图和相应的拼音连接在一起：

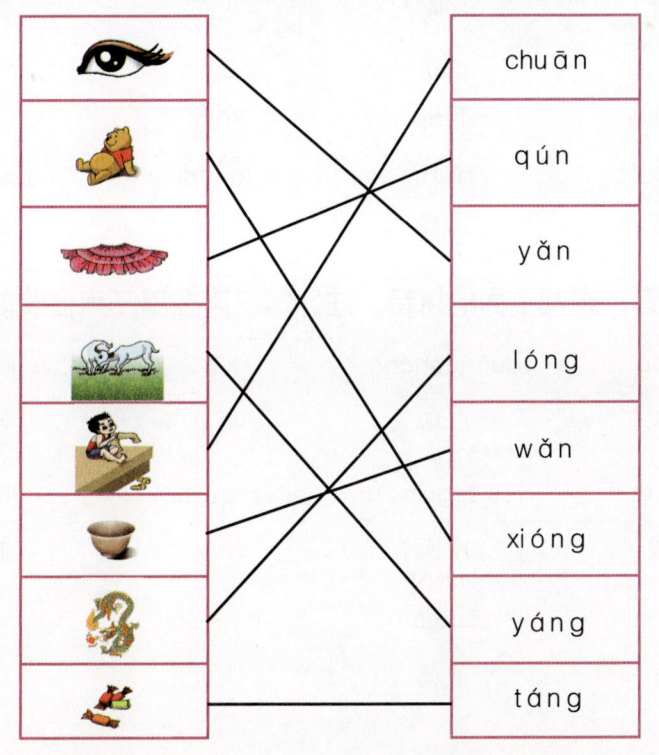

chuān

qún

yǎn

lóng

wǎn

xióng

yáng

táng

九、将下面表格中缺少的韵母填上：

	o			
		ou		
		iou		
		uei		
	in			ün
		iong		

第11课

一、听录音，跟读下面的拼音，注意第三声在非第三声音节前的变调：

lǎoshī	hǎochī	huǒchē	mǔqīn
老师	好吃	火车	母亲
kěnéng	qǐlái	xiǎoshí	yǐqián
可能	起来	小时	以前
guǎnggào	bǐsài	fǎnduì	fǎngwèn
广告	比赛	反对	访问

二、听录音，跟读下面的拼音，注意第三声在第三声音节前的变调：

dǎrǎo	guǎngchǎng	kěyǐ	liǎojiě
打扰	广场	可以	了解
lǎobǎn	lěngyǐn	shǒuzhǐ	yǔsǎn
老板	冷饮	手纸	雨伞
zhǐhǎo	zǎodiǎn	yǒngyuǎn	yǒuhǎo
只好	早点	永远	友好

三、听录音，跟读下面的拼音，注意三个第三声音节连读的变调：

mǎi bǎoxiǎn	zhǎo fǔdǎo	jiǎng yǔfǎ	wǒ xiǎng nǐ
买保险	找辅导	讲语法	我想你
chǔlǐpǐn	guǎnlǐzhě	lǎobǎnyǐ	gǎnjǐn zǒu
处理品	管理者	老板椅	赶紧走

第七课

一、听录音，跟读下面的汉语拼音字母：

b	p	m	f		d	t	n	l
g	k	h			j	q	x	
zh	ch	sh	r		z	c	s	

a	ai	an	ang	ao				
o	ong	ou						
e	ei	en	eng					
i	ia	ian	iang	iao	ie	in	ing	iong	iou
u	ua	uai	uan	uang	uei	uen	ueng	uo
ü	üe	üan	ün					

二、听写拼音（包括声调），注意 y、w 的使用：

1. yú	2. wǒ	3. yǒng	4. wéi	5. yuè	6. yán	7. wài	8. yún
9. wàng	10. yuǎn	11. yè	12. yǎo	13. wēng	14. yìn	15. yá	16. wèn

三、听录音，在与听到的拼音一致的答案后面画√：

1.	gè		kè		guò	√	kuò	
2.	gǒng		jiǒng	√	zhǒng		zǒng	
3.	rì	√	lì		shì		rè	
4.	huā		fā	√	hā		huō	
5.	tè		duò		tuò	√	ruò	
6.	cáng		chán		cán	√	cháng	
7.	bīn		bēng		bīng		bēn	
8.	gōng		gēng		kōng	√	kēng	
9.	cì		cù		sì	√	sù	
10.	jiāo	√	zhāo		qiāo		chāo	
11.	qù		jù	√	qì		jì	
12.	zì		jì		rì		zhì	√

四、听录音，将下面拼音中缺少的声母补上：

1.	zhài	2.	féi	3.	bān	4.	tòu	5.	cáng
6.	pǎo	7.	nüè	8.	hūn	9.	luàn	10.	diǎ
11.	guò	12.	chuāi	13.	xiǔ	14.	ruì	15.	shuā

五、听录音，将下列拼音中缺少的复韵母补上并加上声调：

1.	zuǐ	2.	shuài	3.	nuò	4.	tiē	5.	piào
6.	gěi	7.	fǒu	8.	zhuā	9.	què	10.	jiǒng
11.	huāng	12.	liǎ	13.	xiǔ	14.	chuán	15.	dūn

六、将下面图表中的声母、韵母和声调拼合在一起，组成完整的拼音：

1.	q	iou	-	qiū	6.	x	üan	-	xuān
2.	j	iao	´	jiào	7.	h	uei	`	huì
3.	sh	ou	`	shòu	8.	l	ie	ˇ	liě
4.	x	ün	´	xún	9.	n	üe	`	nüè
5.	k	uen	`	kùn	10.	m	ei	´	méi

第15课

一、听录音，跟读下面的拼音，注意"一"的变调：

yíbàn	yídào	yìbiān	yìqí
一半	一道	一边	一齐

yìshēng	yìtóng	yízài	yìkǒuqì
一生	一同	一再	一口气

二、听录音，跟读下面的拼音，注意"不"的变调：

búduàn	bùguǎn	búlùn	bùgǎndāng
不断	不管	不论	不敢当

bùxǔ	búshì	búguò	búyàojǐn
不许	不是	不过	不要紧

三、听录音，给下面音节中的"yi"加上声调：

yílù shùnfēng	yìjǔ liǎngdé	yírì sānqiū
一路顺风	一举两得	一日三秋

yíshìtóngrén	yìfānfēngshùn	yìxīn yíyì
一视同仁	一帆风顺	一心一意

四、听录音，给下面音节中的"bu"加上声调：

bùcí érbié	bùxiāngshàngxià	shuōyī búèr
不辞而别	不相上下	说一不二

qíngbúzìjīn	bùzhī bùjué	bùbēi búkàng
情不自禁	不知不觉	不卑不亢

五、按照"一"的变调规则，给下面音节中的"yi"加上声调：

yìzhāo yìxī	yìmúyíyàng	yìdiǎn yìdī
一朝一夕	一模一样	一点一滴
yíwèn yìdá	yìshēng yíshì	yìsī yìháo
一问一答	一生一世	一丝一毫

六、按照"不"的变调规则，给下面音节中的"bu"加上声调：

bùduō bùshǎo	bùféi búshòu	bùzhé búkòu
不多不少	不肥不瘦	不折不扣
bújiàn búsàn	bùyán bùyǔ	bùlěng búrè
不见不散	不言不语	不冷不热

七、请按照实际发音修正下面音节中的"一"和"不"的标音：

yíxìliè	yìtiáoxīn	yìlǎnbiǎo
一系列	一条心	一览表
yībǎshǒu	yícìxìng	yī shì yī, èr shì èr
一把手	一次性	一是一，二是二
búxiànghuà	bùdéyǐ	bú'èrjià
不像话	不得已	不二价
búxiùgāng	búyàoliǎn	búzàihu
不锈钢	不要脸	不在乎

八、朗读下面的字谜，注意"不"的读音，并猜猜是什么字：

谜底：林

第17课

一、听录音，跟读下面的拼音，注意"er"的发音：

dīnéng'ér	tuō'érsuǒ	hēimù'ěr	értóngjié
低能儿	托儿所	黑木耳	儿童节
shǔyī shǔ'èr	shuōyī bú'èr	sānxīn'èryì	jiē'èr liánsān
数一数二	说一不二	三心二意	接二连三

二、听录音，跟读下面的拼音，注意韵母尾音在变成儿化韵时的发音变化：

nǎr	yíxiàr	dàhuǒr	miàntiáor
哪儿	一下儿	大伙儿	面条儿
gèr	zhèr	xífùr	xiǎoliǎngkǒur
个儿	这儿	媳妇儿	小两口儿

三、听录音，跟读下面的拼音，注意韵母变成儿化韵时的发音变化：

zhēnbír	dùqír	méi shìr	zhír
针鼻儿	肚脐儿	没事儿	侄儿
tiāo cìr	guāzǐr	sūnnǚr	xiǎoqǔr
挑刺儿	瓜子儿	孙女儿	小曲儿

四、听录音，跟读下面的拼音，注意韵母尾音在变成儿化韵时的发音变化：

mòshuǐr	yíhuìr	xiǎoháir	míngpáir
墨水儿	一会儿	小孩儿	名牌儿
liángfěnr	shūběnr	niúròugānr	ménkǎnr
凉粉儿	书本儿	牛肉干儿	门槛儿

五、听录音，跟读下面的拼音，注意韵母在变成儿化韵时的发音变化：

càidiér	piě	pèijuér	mùjué
菜碟儿	撇儿	配角儿	木橛儿
duǎnqúnr	bù héqúnr	dàijìnr	bào xìnr
短裙儿	不合群儿	带劲儿	报信儿

六、听录音，跟读下面的拼音，注意韵母在变成儿化韵时的发音变化：

méiyǐngr	yǎnjìngr	shìbǐngr	luósīdīngr
没影儿	眼镜儿	柿饼儿	螺丝钉儿

七、听录音，跟读下面的拼音，注意韵母尾音在变成儿化韵时的发音变化：

shuǐkēngr	xìsǎngr	xiǎoxióngr	hútòngr
水坑儿	细嗓儿	小熊儿	胡同儿

八、听录音，跟读下面的拼音，注意儿化与非儿化词语在词性上的不同：

huó	huór	huǒ	huǒr
活	活儿	火	火儿
bāo	bāor	cì	cìr
包	包儿	刺	刺儿

九、听录音，跟读下面的拼音，注意儿化与非儿化词语在意义上的不同：

xìn	xìnr	nà	nàr
信	信儿	那	那儿
zǎodiǎn	zǎodiǎnr	méijìn	méijìnr
早点	早点儿	没劲	没劲儿

十、听录音，注意儿化音节与非儿化音节意义上的不同：

guógē	míngēr	bówùguǎn	cháguǎnr
国歌	民歌儿	博物馆	茶馆儿
zīběn	jìshìběnr	fāngzhēn	dàtóuzhēnr
资本	记事本儿	方针	大头针儿

十一、听录音，给下面的词语注音：

nǚ'ér	xiànrbǐng	yīng'ér	shuǐjiǎor
女儿	馅儿饼	婴儿	水饺儿
liáo tiānr	hǎowánr	érnǚ	wányìr
聊天儿	好玩儿	儿女	玩意儿

第十课

一、听录音，跟读下面的拼音，注意轻声音节的发音：

dōngxi	xiāoxi	gūniang	qīngchu
东西	消息	姑娘	清楚
háizi	piányi	késou	liángkuai
孩子	便宜	咳嗽	凉快
xǐhuan	wǎnshang	nǐmen	nuǎnhuo
喜欢	晚上	你们	暖和
mǎhu	ěrduo	jiǎozi	shěnshen
马虎	耳朵	饺子	婶婶
màozi	àiren	piàoliang	dàifu
帽子	爱人	漂亮	大夫

二、听录音，跟读下面的拼音，注意亲属称呼的正确读音：

bàba	māma	yéye	nǎinai
爸爸	妈妈	爷爷	奶奶
bóbo	shūshu	gūgu	jiùjiu
伯伯	叔叔	姑姑	舅舅
gēge	dìdi	jiějie	mèimei
哥哥	弟弟	姐姐	妹妹

三、听录音，跟读下面的拼音，对比画线词语的读音：

xǐhuan	liánhuān	yīfu	xīfú
喜欢	联欢	衣服	西服
mántou	jìngtóu	shíhou	děnghòu
馒头	镜头	时候	等候
àiren	qíngrén	bùfen	bǐfēn
爱人	情人	部分	比分
fúqi	nuǎnqì	yìsi	xiāngsī
福气	暖气	意思	相思

四、听录音，跟读下面的拼音，注意同一词语的不同读法：

dìfang	dìfāng	rénjia	rénjiā
地方	地方	人家	人家
jīngshen	jīngshén	dàyi	dàyì
精神	精神	大意	大意
yányu	yányǔ	lìhai	lìhài
言语	言语	利害	利害

趣味汉语拼音课本（基础篇）

五、听录音，在与听到的拼音一致的答案后面画√：

1	běnshi	√	běnshì		6	rényi		rényì	√
2	fǎnzhèng		fǎnzheng	√	7	xiàshui	√	xiàshuǐ	
3	gàosù		gàosu	√	8	xiǎozǐ		xiǎozi	√
4	gùshi	√	gùshì		9	zhàoying	√	zhàoyìng	
5	méndào	√	méndao		10	xiōngdi		xiōngdì	√

六、听录音，给下面的拼音加上声调，注意拼音中的轻声：

zhàngfu	yǒuyì	yīnwèi	xièxie
xiǎohár	tiānqì	zìjǐ	wǎnshang
shōushi	shūfu	nǚ'ér	máfan

131